YOUR PRESIDENTIAL FANTASY DREAM TEAM

YOUR PRESIDENTIAL FANTASY DREAM TEAM

DANIEL O'BRIEN

Illustrated by Winston Rowntree

♕

CROWN BOOKS
for YOUNG READERS

NEW YORK

Visit us on the Web! randomhousekids.com

Educators and librarians, for a variety of teaching tools,
visit us at RHTeachersLibrarians.com

Library of Congress Cataloging-in-Publication Data
Names: O'Brien, Daniel. | Rowntree, Winston, illustrator.
Title: Your presidential fantasy dream team / Daniel O'Brien ; illustrated by Winston Rowntree.
Description: First edition. | New York : Crown, 2016. | Audience: Grades 4 to 6. | Audience: 10+
Identifiers: LCCN 2015030285 | ISBN 978-0-553-53747-5 (tr. pbk.) | ISBN 978-0-553-53748-2 (glb) |
ISBN 978-0-553-53749-9 (epub)
Subjects: LCSH: Presidents—United States—Humor—Juvenile literature. | United States—Politics and
government—Humor—Juvenile literature. | American wit and humor—Juvenile literature.
Classification: LCC E176.1 .O279 2016 | DDC 352.23/80973—dc23

Printed in the United States of America
10 9 8 7 6 5 4 3 2 1
First Edition

THIS BOOK IS DEDICATED TO EVERY ONE
OF MY TEACHERS WHO YELLED AT ME FOR NOT
PAYING ATTENTION IN CLASS. (YOU WERE RIGHT.)

AND FOR ELISE.

CONTENTS

INTRODUCTION

DRAFTING YOUR PRESIDENTIAL FANTASY DREAM TEAM

I can't predict the future. So I'm not saying that several years from now, robots will rise up and attempt to overthrow humanity and it'll be up to you to travel through time and assemble a Presidential Attack Squad to defend America. But I *am* saying that we'd all feel really stupid if at least *one* of us wasn't prepared for such an event. If you're ever tasked with organizing the Dream Team of Presidents, this chapter will probably be more helpful than any other chapter in any book, ever.

Whether you're forming an action team to defend the planet or just putting together a group of presidents to pull off some kind of grand scheme, every good team needs Brains, Brawn, a Loose Cannon, a Moral Compass, and a Roosevelt. I've included my best recommendations for all these positions, but you should feel free to pick your own.

THE BRAINS

Brains are incredibly valuable (one of the reasons zombies want them so much). You need someone who can make a plan and think quickly on his feet just in case that plan falls apart (which, if you're planning something big and elaborate with a lot of moving pieces, it almost certainly will). Without a competent leader running the show, your team will just be a bunch of angry presidents running around without any direction.

My pick: Abraham Lincoln is your man. If you're talking about a guy who won't crumble when the heat's on and everything's falling apart, you want the guy who kept a cool head when the country legitimately fell apart (see page 101). Lincoln didn't even have any military background when he took office, but as soon as the

Civil War broke out, he picked it up *real* quick. He met with generals, he read books on strategy, he talked with his troops and confidently mapped out the North's strategy for victory, and he saw it through.

A good Brains guy sees everything several steps ahead of everyone else, which makes Lincoln—a man who saw the future and predicted his own death—uniquely equipped for the job.

Alternate choice: Theodore Roosevelt

THE BRAWN

Every team needs muscle. The A-Team needed Mr. T, the Avengers needed the Hulk, and Alvin and the Chipmunks needed Mr. T, on that one episode when Mr. T was a guest star ("The C-Team"). For your Mr. T, you're going to want someone strong, tough, and crazy. Someone who doesn't need to be the smartest or the nicest, but who knows how to punch until there's nothing left to punch.

My pick: You need **Andrew Jackson.** There's not much to say about his toughness beyond what's already been said in his chapter (see page 47). Plus I'm worried that if I type his name one more time, he'll appear and challenge me to a duel (the man LOVED duels), and I am *not* prepared for that.

Alternate choice: Theodore Roosevelt

THE LOOSE CANNON

Look, there's no reason to sugarcoat this: every good attack squad needs someone who can do what others can't do, someone who isn't afraid to get his hands dirty. He operates in a moral gray area and might not always follow the law to the letter, but he gets stuff *done.*

My pick: For this position, I cannot give **James K. Polk** a higher recommendation. In the 1840s, the stuff that needed to be got done was American expansion. We needed to stretch out to the Pacific Coast to fulfill our Manifest Destiny, and Polk was the one who made it happen. As you'll learn in the Polk chapter (see page 71), there's evidence that Polk *lied* to make this happen, to make America bigger and

stronger. Did he lie? We don't know for sure, but we DO know that Polk is the kind of man who can make tough decisions in the interest of serving the greater good.
Alternate choice: Theodore Roosevelt

THE MORAL COMPASS

Without a strong Moral Compass, your team could fall under the control of your Brawn and Loose Cannon. You need someone pure steering the ship, a leader everyone can get behind. Without Captain America, the Avengers would be consumed by ego and bouts of one-upmanship. Without Leonardo, the rest of the Teenage Mutant Ninja Turtles would succumb to a life of attitude and pizza parties. Without Moe, the Stooges would be lost in a dark world of violence and banana cream pies. Every group needs a guiding beacon to remind everyone that they're the *good guys*.

My pick: The obvious choice for your team is **George Washington,** who is basically already Captain America to begin with. Washington is the only president that no other president has dared to criticize or find fault with; he's the only man who could rein in the egos and personalities of the rest of the team and keep them in check.
Alternate choice: Theodore Roosevelt

THE ROOSEVELT

Without a good Roosevelt, your team might as well just stay home, because they'd be as good as dead out in the field. The Roosevelt of your team will bring courage, spirit, adaptability, and a certain "Rooseveltiness" that no other presidents can equal.

My pick: For this position, I recommend **Theodore Roosevelt.**
Alternate choice: Theodore Roosevelt.
　　Look, I'm not budging on this. If there really IS a robot uprising, you can bet that the robots built a robo–Theodore Roosevelt ("Theodore Robosevelt"), and if you don't have the real deal on your side, you won't stand a chance. Roosevelt embodies every other archetype on this list, and you'd be stupid not to have him. I

guess you could maybe swap him out for Franklin Roosevelt, who is at an advantage by already being part robot, but if TR's free, your choice should be pretty clear. All Teddy, all day.

But again, these are only *my* top choices for the positions, if *I* was the one tasked with building this team. This book will provide you with lots of information about presidents, plenty enough for you to decide for yourself what the best Dream Team configuration might be. You might decide that you'd rather have William McKinley as your Brawn because he's so big, or you might want Millard Fillmore on your squad for some bizarre reason that escapes me. But that's you, and that's your choice. I'm just here to give you the facts you need to make your decisions.

Here's a scorecard so you can decide whether to draft each president to a spot on your Fantasy Dream Team. I suggest you make a copy of the scorecard, in case you change your mind as you read other chapters. This is an even better idea if you've borrowed this book from a friend or the library.

THE PRESIDENTIAL ★ SCORECARD

Brains 🎓	
Brawn 🏋	
Loose Cannon 🧨	
Moral Compass ⚖	
Roosevelt... 🥽	

★ 1 ★
GEORGE WASHINGTON

THE PRESIDENT OF PRESIDENTS

Presidential Term: 1789–1797
Political Party: None
Spouse: Martha Dandridge
Children: None, though he's technically the
Father of His Country, so . . . lots?
Birthdate: February 22, 1732
Death Date: December 14, 1799
Fun Fact: Washington is literally on money.

There are two kinds of people in this world: people who don't actively enjoy being shot at, and George Washington. Most of you are probably in that first group, and that's why no one will ever put your picture on money.

The idea that Washington liked being shot at isn't up for debate, mind you. No one is saying that Washington *probably* enjoyed being shot at because of his willingness to return to battle in service of his country; he *admitted* to it. In a letter to his brother about his time on the battlefield, Washington said, "I heard the bullets whistle, and, believe me, there is something charming in the sound," which, according to rumor, prompted King George III to remark that Washington's attitude would change if he'd heard a few more. *"Oh ho ho, perhaps you're right,"* Washington may have said good-naturedly with a chuckle, before he absolutely destroyed King George's entire army and ran America for eight glorious and strong-jawed years.

But we know all that already. We all know how tough and noble Washington was. If you studied Washington at all in school, you know that he was a good man and a just president, a friend to everyone and everything (with the notable exception, according to some rumors, of cherry trees). We know all of this because everyone talks about how bright, strong, and fair President George Washington was. But I'm going to talk about how he was also probably *magic*.

Let's start with how Washington knew America was going to war before America even had an *army*. Sure, the seeds of discontent had already been sown, but war was not a foregone conclusion to anyone but Washington even in 1775, when the Continental Congress met for the second time to discuss what to do about Great Britain's unfair taxation practices. War was an *option*, but not a certainty at that point, at least not in the eyes of the members of the Continental Congress. Many of the Founding Fathers, like Benjamin Franklin, still had great fondness for their mother country, and they were eager to find a peaceful solution with the homeland.

But not Washington. Whether he could see the future and knew war was coming or he simply *willed* the war into existence, Washington was ahead of the curve. On his way to the meeting (before war had been declared—or even discussed—and before he'd been given command of the Continental Army), he stopped off to buy some books about war strategy, tomahawks, and new holsters for his guns. If that didn't send a clear-enough message, he showed up to the meeting *already wearing his military uniform,* while the rest of the representatives were trying to handle this whole "revolution thing" delicately and diplomatically. It was like everyone else at the meeting was discussing whether or not they should build a bomb, and Washington had already lit the fuse. It wasn't just about finding another chance to challenge a bunch of bullets to a game of chicken (though it's true Washington never missed an opportunity to do so). He knew war was inevitable and wanted to be dressed appropriately.

And of course, Washington was right. War *was* necessary. Even if it wasn't necessary before, it was necessary *because* he said it was. For reasons that will never be clear to historians (but will be to people who accept magic as a possibility), the universe bends to Washington's will.

Here's one of the most important things you need to know about Washington:

he should not have been able to lead America to victory in the Revolutionary War. When it came time to choose someone to command the Continental Army, Washington was chosen for his *popularity,* not his skills as a general. He was brave and a great soldier, but he'd never commanded anything larger than a regiment, and when he'd been handed an entire army of untrained, undisciplined troops, he started messing up almost immediately. He lost more battles than he won, and the majority of those losses were a direct result of his own arrogance and over-aggressiveness. Yes, Washington—the man we all like to remember as the quiet, dignified, reluctant soldier—was a short-tempered fighter who never turned down a battle. If you think that never turning down a battle despite your army being terrible and untrained is a bad strategy, congratulations, you'd make a better general than George Washington. (Feel free to brag to all your friends.)

Unlike most soldiers (and, indeed, most sane human beings), Washington didn't see a battle as a means to an end, or as an unfortunate but necessary part of achieving important goals. He saw it as a chance to show his enemies how brave and strong he and his army were. He'd treat every challenge from his opponents not like a necessary evil that needed to be stopped as quickly as possible, but like a personal attack on him, as if the opposing army were just pointing at Washington and bawking like a chicken. After being called a chicken, instead of calmly using the timeless and brilliant "I'm rubber and you're glue" strategy, Washington over-reacted and sent his exhausted and unskilled army after every insult. In case you've never led an army before, you should know that this is a bad strategy, especially when your opponent is stronger, larger, and more experienced, as Great Britain was.

This overaggressive strategy blew up in Washington's face over and over again. At many times during the war, it seemed that America's favorite son was too arrogant and reckless to bring us to victory. Indeed, Washington rarely *won* battles; he mostly just survived using "strategic retreat." If that sounds like a fancy, classy way of saying "running away," that's because it *is.*

So how did it happen? How did an inexperienced commander with an unfocused and untrained army equipped with a mostly "run away bravely" approach to warfare win the most important war in American history? The short answer, again, is "probably magic." Washington firmly believed that Providence or fate was on his side, in everything he did. In the way that war was declared because Washington walked into a room and *said* war was declared, Washington won the war because he *said* he was going to. That's how Washington could look at loss after loss and think, *Huh, that's weird. I'm supposed to win. I guess no one told that to these guys. No matter, I'll just go ahead and win it now.* And he did.

Not overnight, obviously. Washington gradually became a much better commander, which probably comes as no surprise to you because you know that (spoiler alert) America won its independence and we named a TON of stuff after Washington.

Washington's tyranny of will didn't just determine the outcome of the war, it also saved his life. Washington would return from many battles unharmed, but with bullet holes in his clothing, or without a horse. (Two different horses were shot out from under Washington *twice in the same battle.*) This happened so many times that George Washington proclaimed on more than one occasion that he could not be killed in battle. He genuinely believed this. And the crazy part? *We have no way to prove him wrong.*

That's how a first-time commander won a war against the most powerful army and navy in the world: Sheer. Blind. Belief. Washington said he was going to win, and he did. His strategic retreat policy ended up really paying off. Washington knew that he was outnumbered and that his enemy had better training, but he *also* knew that his enemy had to deal with the annoying cost of shipping thousands of soldiers across the sea to fight. The smartest thing Washington could do was just keep his army alive and around. As long as they were actively fighting, Great Britain would have to maintain its presence and keep up this very expensive war, even if Washington's troops kept running away.

In the winter of 1777, Washington brought his army to a military camp in Pennsylvania (Valley Forge). Back then, it was generally understood that battles would mostly only be waged from spring to autumn, with all armies generally agreeing that winter was just too cold for fighting. This meant that Washington had a few months at Valley Forge to regroup without fearing any attack from the British. While his enemies were relaxing up in Philadelphia, with heat and plenty of food,

Washington recruited Baron Friedrich Wilhelm von Steuben, a very experienced Prussian drillmaster, to train the ragtag Continental Army into a fearsome fighting machine. They entered Valley Forge sick, cold, exhausted, and with close to no resources (many of the soldiers didn't even have shoes), but thanks to Washington and Baron von Steuben, they came out the other side trained, rested, and *ready*. And not only did the soldiers now have more supplies and resources, but they also had the added confidence of having just survived one of the worst winters of their lives; they were tough and they knew it. After that, the British didn't really stand a chance.

You know the rest. America won the war; Washington became the first and so far only president elected unanimously; and he and his wife, Martha, got to work

on running America. Martha was a perfect match for George—charming and serious and noble, and at all times completely aware of the import of what her husband and she were doing together. A lot of people at the time said that George's smartest political move was marrying Martha, who came from a great family and was the richest woman in Virginia when they met. Marrying Martha raised Washington's own status, increased his wealth, and made him a member of the aristocracy. Like everything else George and Martha did, it also set an interesting precedent. George married the richest woman in town, and since then, not one president has ever married beneath his station. (Most have married above.) Our presidents, even the notoriously humble ones like Abraham "Log Cabin" Lincoln, went after aristocrats and the daughters of the richest parents in town. (Lyndon Johnson exclusively courted the daughters of the three richest men in Texas.) Some presidents fell in *love* with women beneath their station, but they didn't marry them. Does this speak to a broader trend about presidents always trying to marry up in an obsessive quest for power and status, or did everyone else just copy Washington because he was so cool and they wanted to impress his ghost? The world may never know (but probably the first thing).

Washington's presidency was both underwhelming and overwhelming. On the one hand, nothing HUGE happened—America wasn't invaded by outside attackers, there wasn't a natural disaster, and there wasn't a huge national strike of any kind. There was no Civil War or economic collapse or any of the other "big moments" that can define most presidencies. On the other hand, *everything that happened was huge,* because everything Washington did set a precedent, because it was the first time any president did it. He served two terms because he *felt* like only serving two terms, and that's why there's a two-term limit today (exceeded only once, by FDR, before it became an official law). He created a cabinet with the offices of the secretary of state, the secretary of the treasury, the secretary of war, and the attorney general, and we still have those jobs today. He came up with the idea of a cabinet because having a group of trusted advisors, all with very different opinions, appealed to him, and we have never looked back. In his farewell address to the nation before leaving office, he cautioned against getting too involved and wrapped up in the affairs of other countries, and he urged people to focus on maintaining America's strength and individualism. That set the tone for foreign affairs in America *forever*. We are STILL hearing echoes of that sentiment today. Everything Washington did was a first, and we all listened carefully because EVERYONE listens to Washington.

Even Death waited on Washington's orders before finally claiming his soul for that big battlefield in the sky. In December of 1799, Washington fell ill and a team of doctors tried for hours to restore his health. Having decided that he'd spent enough time being the best at being alive, Washington decided to try his hand at fighting ghosts, and he sent the doctors away, telling them to give up. The doctors could have at least *tried* to keep him alive for a little bit longer, but Washington had had enough. On his deathbed, Washington told his aide, Tobias Lear, "I am just going," and he died *while taking his own pulse.* You can almost see Death quietly sitting in Washington's room, waiting for permission to take his life.

You'd be crazy not to want Washington on your Presidential Fantasy Dream Team. Not only is he one of the tougher, luckier, and more magical presidents, but it's also pretty likely that Washington is the only man capable of leading a team of action presidents. If you're building an elite squad of accomplished heroes with enormous egos, you're going to want someone with the ability to command ANY-ONE'S respect at the helm. Washington is your man.

OFFICIAL FANTASY DREAM TEAM RATING

Not including Washington is a MONUMENTALLY bad idea. He's a pretty good fit for most positions, but my suggestion is making him your **Moral Compass.** The other presidents on your Fantasy Dream Team will be tougher or smarter, and they will all CERTAINLY have huge egos; they need a man like Washington guiding them, rallying them, and leading them into whatever battle they have to face.

THE PRESIDENTIAL ★ SCORECARD

? Brains
? Brawn
? Loose Cannon
? Moral Compass
? Roosevelt...

2

JOHN ADAMS

THE CEREBRAL ASSASSIN

Presidential Term: 1797–1801
Political Party: Federalist
Spouse: Abigail Smith
Children: Abigail ("Nabby"), John Quincy (more on him later),
Susanna, Charles, and Thomas
Birthdate: October 30, 1735
Death Date: July 4, 1826
Fun Fact: Adams hated fun and loved facts.

Let's get this out of the way: our first vice president and second president of the United States of America, John Adams, is much, much smarter than you. He's not the *toughest* guy in the world (we'll get to Teddy Roosevelt later), but he had one of the greatest minds of any president in history, and he regularly used that mind to accomplish seemingly impossible tasks. Adams dedicated his mind to fighting and winning the hardest and most uphill battles he could find.

In 1770, members of the British Army shot and killed five civilian men in what came to be known as the Boston Massacre. To provide some context, Bostonians in the late 1700s did not have a ton of love for the British. They saw their British rulers as oppressors, and influential Bostonians were starting to whisper about an American Revolution before the rest of the country had even considered it. Bostonians were already looking for more excuses to hate the British, so to them, the Boston Massacre wasn't just a tragedy; it was an opportunity to paint the British as reckless, violent oppressors. The British soldiers were destined to face trial, but no lawyer in Boston would represent them in court because everyone knew that whoever defended the horrible British would (a) probably lose and (b) certainly be despised by the rest of the British-hating Bostonians.

John Adams was not a man who cared about being hated. Much like the thousands of reality television stars who would eventually fill the beautiful country he worked so hard to build, he didn't come here to make friends. He loved humanity but didn't care for people, and never quite figured out how to relate to and interact with them. He cared about his legacy and getting proper credit for his accomplishments, but he didn't care about fame or popularity; having principles and sticking to them was all that interested Adams. He had his ideals, his beliefs, and his convictions, and he wasn't shy about sharing them. Being righteous wasn't just more important than being friendly or considerate; to Adams, it was *everything*.

That's why he took the Boston Massacre case that every other lawyer stayed away from. There was no better way to represent his "being righteous is more important than having friends" philosophy than by defending the British soldiers in the Boston Massacre trial.

It would be convenient for us to believe that the British were needlessly cruel and evil, heartlessly firing shots at the poor, innocent Bostonians, but the less flattering truth is that the "innocent" civilians provoked the attack. They confronted the British in the form of a rowdy, unruly mob armed with clubs, and hurled garbage and insults in equal measure. Most *suggested* that the British start firing upon them. That's how much the people of Boston hated the British—they begged to be shot just so they'd have an excuse to demand independence. Many townsfolk later went to the post-Massacre trial to intimidate the witnesses into testifying against the British. Now the soldiers were facing trial with a jury *full* of Bostonians, and if that wasn't enough, the witnesses were being tampered with.

John Adams won that case. That's how good he is. That's how *smart* he is. If Adams believes he's in the right, then absolutely *nothing* will stop him from accomplishing his goals. Boston was a ticking time bomb of anti-British rhetoric, and Adams convinced an entire courtroom that the soldiers who shot and killed five civilians were in the *right*.

Adams continued his streak of fighting tough fights four years later at the Continental Congress, where he faced the uphill battle of convincing every other representative of the thirteen colonies that a revolution was necessary. Almost *everyone* wanted to negotiate with the British peacefully and avoid war at absolutely all costs. Only Adams and Washington knew for sure that a violent revolution was not just necessary but needed to happen *immediately.* Adams did it with his giant, terrifying brain. Richard Stockton, New Jersey's representative to the Congress, called Adams the Atlas of American Independence because of his dedication to carrying this cause on his back. You see, the Continental Congress was like a big street brawl, except instead of fighting with hands and feet, opposing sides traded long, passionate monologues. You can call it "word-fighting" (or simply "talking" if you're a square), and Adams was the best word-fighter around. His speeches in favor of independence were so heartfelt and convincing that he reduced grown men to tears. His most outspoken opponent in the Continental Congress, Pennsylvania's John Dickinson, was so devastated by John Adams's skill as a word-fighter that he resigned his position and joined the Pennsylvania militia. Dickinson was the guy who never wanted to resort to war and wanted peace with Great Britain more than anything, but Adams's argument was so moving that he quit and picked up a gun against them.

To put it simply, Adams just knew how to think and speak better than every-one. He knew how to get inside people's heads because he paid attention. When-ever he met new people, he'd go home and write about them in his diary—how tall they were, what their hobbies were, what their strengths were, what their flaws were. Adams was an observer, and he used the information he gathered to cut to the core of people. He knew men well enough to know what they needed to hear to see his point of view, and if they *refused* to join his side, he would take their biggest insecurity and shine the brightest spotlight on it for everyone to see.

It might seem hard to believe, but Adams wasn't popular *even when he was president.* He was respected enough to be made president in the first place, but he never quite got the hang of popularity. After the American Revolution, America and Great Britain were working toward mending old wounds to keep trade going, but Great Britain was still at war with France. France started seizing American merchant ships that were trading with the British as punishment. Adams's po-litical party, the Federalists, wanted America to get involved to help the British, but Thomas Jefferson, his vice president, wanted America to step in and support France. Most Americans, meanwhile, just wanted to go to war. So Adams was faced with two options—one his party would love or one his vice president would love—and he STILL managed to go with the option that would make him the least popu-lar: he sent a diplomat to France in 1799 to broker a peace deal. He got France to agree to stop harassing American ships and kept America out of another war that would have been as costly as it was impossible to win. Making peace with France was *absolutely* the right move, but, like almost everything else that Adams did in the interest of being right, this dramatically hurt his popularity and divided the Federalists. He was so proud of his ability to make peace with France that he actu-ally had that accomplishment engraved on his tombstone (obviously leaving out the fact that this unpopular decision contributed to his inability to get reelected for a second term). He was the first president to serve only one term—a tradition that would be carried on by his son, John Quincy, a few years later.

Probably the only person who always really liked John Adams was his wife, Abigail (which is a great quality to have in a wife). Like Martha Washington before her, Abigail was a perfect match for her husband—wise, kind, dedicated, and moral. Unlike

Martha (and, indeed, many First Ladies to come), Abigail was less interested in the hosting and ceremonial duties of being the First Lady and much more interested in the world of politics, and she served as both a confidante and an advisor to her president, counseling him as much as his own cabinet. This wasn't a typical eighteenth-century marriage with the man being king of the castle and the woman quietly busying herself with domestic life; John and Abigail were true partners who loved and respected each other. (He called her "his best and wisest advisor.") John encouraged Abigail's studies and never shied away from praising her intelligence or political instincts.

Adams was always an underdog. He was never a soldier (even though he would often tell his wife that he was jealous that Washington got to go out and fight battles while he had to stick around boring Philadelphia shaping the modern idea of democracy), and physically, there's nothing too impressive about him. He smoked, he was overweight, he was short (five feet seven inches), he had lost most of his teeth by the time he became president, and his hands shook. Despite all that, Adams lived to be over ninety years old *in the 1800s,* back when most people died by fifty.

OFFICIAL FANTASY DREAM TEAM RATING

You're going to want a man like Adams on your Presidential Fantasy Dream Team because of that giant, terrifying brain of his. Plenty of presidents have been stronger, healthier, cooler, and more Rooseveltian, but few have been able to focus on doing what's right quite like Adams. He's not popular, but you're not running a popularity contest, and when and if the world starts to collapse around you, you're going to want someone who can make the right decision in the face of disaster, disagreement, and outright hostility. (His ability to make his opponents weep probably won't hurt either.) He'd be a great fit for either your **Brains** or **Moral Compass** position. The rest of your team may dislike him, but darn it, they will *respect* him when he's right.

3

THOMAS JEFFERSON

JUST INVENTED SIX DIFFERENT DEVICES WHILE YOU READ THIS

Presidential Term: 1801–1809
Political Party: Democratic-Republican
Spouse: Martha Wayles
Children: Martha, Jane, Mary, Lucy, and Lucy Elizabeth.
Only Martha and Mary survived to adulthood.
Birthdate: April 13, 1743
Death Date: July 4, 1826
Fun Fact: Jefferson had no idea how to dress himself,
so he looked like an idiot almost all the time.

The worst crime I could commit as the author of this book would be to let the brilliance of Thomas Jefferson's mind and the eloquence of his pen overshadow what a top-to-bottom, no-holds-barred, unflinching tough guy he was.

Jefferson *was* a great thinker, and he *did* make a greater impact on American politics than any other person in history, but he was also supremely cool—a fact that is rarely brought up in history classes. It's not *just* that Jefferson wrote the Declaration of Independence—the single most important American document ever printed (until now!)—and it's not *just* that he personally invented more useful and lasting devices than any president before or since; Jefferson was one cold, cool, collected dude with a taste for rebellion.

Jefferson truly believed that a country couldn't preserve its liberties if its leaders weren't regularly warned that the people could rise up and take the government down. He not only believed that the people should always be ready to question and threaten the authority with violence, but he also encouraged it, *even though he was the authority*! He basically took the office and challenged all comers to take him on.

But Jefferson wasn't just about straight-up *begging* for a rebellion on his own soil (and encouraging future generations of informed Americans to take up arms whenever their freedoms are threatened), he also knew how to protect America abroad. For fifteen straight years, America was paying anywhere from $80,000 to $1 million every year to the Barbary States in exchange for protection from North African pirates. It was basically a shakedown; if you wanted to trade anywhere in the Caribbean, the Barbary States wanted you to pay "tribute," and as long as the checks cleared, the pirates wouldn't hassle your ships. For a while, everyone paid the pirates off.

All of that stopped on a dime (or nickel!) when Jefferson took office. As an inauguration present, the Barbary States sent Jefferson a demand for over $200,000 from the new administration, and Jefferson responded with the nineteenth-century version of "Bite me, pirates." The pirates responded with the nineteenth-century version of "No," which meant they declared war on America.

Now, at this time, it wasn't really clear *what* powers a president had when it came to war or defending the country. America was still new enough that we didn't yet have a system in place, and the Constitution wasn't super clear, but that didn't stop Jefferson from sending out the newly formed U.S. Navy. Jefferson didn't *ask;* he told Congress, "I communicate [to you] all material information on this subject . . . I instruct[ed] the commanders of armed American vessels to seize all vessels and goods of [those idiotic pirates]." Congress was welcome to sit around and figure out exactly what he was allowed to do, and in the meantime, he already went ahead and sent out his navy to just wreck house on those pirates.

And wreck house they did. The war between America and the pirates became known as the First Barbary War. It was fought at sea and in the Barbary States (what is today North Africa), was quickly won by the Americans, and was the first time in history that the United States flag was raised on foreign land. It was also proof that America could command and win a war from home, and proof that the strength of the American military was not *just* reserved for the easy-to-fight-for

cause of independence. This was a military that knew how to fight *together,* under one flag. And who rallied those troops and made this war happen? Who started and ended a war in *just one presidential term*? Jefferson.

Still, don't let Jefferson's image as an action hero overshadow the strength of his brilliant mind. He perfected designs for the plow, the macaroni machine, the polygraph, and the dumbwaiter, and he invented and built the portable copying press, the revolving chair, and the pedometer. We know he invented these things because he wrote about it in letters and his journal, but he never sought patents for any of them. This isn't included in this chapter to make you feel inferior (though, yes, you should); it's included because *someone* needs to give Jefferson credit for his inventions. Jefferson didn't think anyone should hold a patent for an invention, so he never once filed for a patent, even though inventing was sort of his thing. These are the actions of a man guided by principle, and a man guided by principle is either incredibly dangerous or a huge asset, depending on whose side he's on. And, really, if Jefferson's not on your side, guess what: *you're on the wrong side.*

Do you live in Arkansas, Missouri, Iowa, Oklahoma, Kansas, Nebraska, Minnesota, North Dakota, South Dakota, New Mexico, Texas, Colorado, or Louisiana? If you don't live there, do you at least appreciate that America has them? Well, you've got Jefferson to thank. He was the one who negotiated with France to acquire the Louisiana Purchase, a territory that included all or part of these states. Jefferson had a thirst for expanding and exploring America, which is why he also commissioned the Lewis and Clark Expedition in 1804. The Lewis and Clark Expedition was the first American exploration into the West, sending explorers all the way to the Pacific Coast to learn about the land and its plant and animal life, and to establish an American presence all over the country as soon as possible.

Of course, Jefferson wouldn't be a rad president if he didn't run his own life with the same iron fist he used to run America. Jefferson liked being in control, and his death was no exception. Jefferson had been sick for almost a full year before being committed to his deathbed. On July 3, 1826, when Jefferson knew his time was almost up, he gave strict instructions for exactly how he wanted his funeral to go (no parade, no celebration), and then wordlessly held out for *seventeen more hours* specifically so he could die on the Fourth of July, for the fiftieth anniversary of the Declaration of Independence. Jefferson wanted a dramatic exit. He had a plan, and he wasn't going to let something as silly as old age, kidney failure, or pneumonia get in the way. As a bizarre footnote, he died at almost the exact same moment John Adams died. Adams and Jefferson started out as very close friends but then became political rivals. Toward the end of their lives, they briefly rekindled their friendship, but there was always some degree of competition between them. Adams, who, like Jefferson, died on the fiftieth anniversary of the Fourth of July, chose as his last words: "Thomas Jefferson still survives." In reality, Jefferson had actually died a few hours BEFORE Adams, but the news hadn't reached Adams. It's a bizarre coincidence, sure, but also just one more chance for Jefferson to prove Adams wrong, even in death. Adams would have hated (but respected) that.

Even Thomas Jefferson's final resting place is impressive. It's fitting that he left detailed instructions regarding his tombstone. He designed his own marker and demanded that it read "Here was buried Thomas Jefferson, Author of the Declaration of American Independence, of the Statute of Virginia for religious freedom, Father of the University of Virginia." Notice anything missing? At the time of his death, Jefferson was one of only *six human beings in history* to serve as president of the United States of America, but he was so casual about this fact that he explicitly told people not to include it on his tombstone because it just wasn't a big deal to him.

OFFICIAL FANTASY DREAM TEAM RATING

A talent like Jefferson is as rare as a two-dollar bill; recruit him! His intelligence and constant search for knowledge and information make him a great fit for your **Brains.**

4

JAMES MADISON

THE TINY NIGHTMARE

Presidential Term: 1809–1817

Political Party: Democratic-Republican

Spouse: Dolley Payne Todd

Children: John

Birthdate: March 16, 1751

Death Date: June 28, 1836

Fun Fact: At five feet four inches, Madison is the smallest president we have ever had or will ever have. I mean it. I will bet $10,000 that we will never elect a shorter president from now until the world explodes.

In his lifetime, James Madison was called the Father of the Constitution by his peers, and while the importance of his role in shaping the laws that govern our country cannot be overstated, they *really* should have called him Tiny Impossible Nightmare. But they didn't, because none of the people who gave out nicknames in the 1700s were as good at it as I am.

Sure, Madison had one of the sharpest political minds America would ever have access to, but to understand how impressive Madison was, we need to spend some time talking about how terrible he was. Madison's life was defined by being great at the things he was supposed to be bad at. He looked like anything BUT a president—he was five feet four inches and only broke one hundred pounds on his *best day* and before his midafternoon poop. His speaking voice was high and weak, so much so that reporters who came to see him speak often left blanks in their transcripts when they couldn't hear him or simply gave up out of frustration.

The man was a *president,* but his voice was so weak and annoying that reporters just couldn't be bothered.

It wasn't just that Madison's *voice* was awful; for a very long time, the things he used his voice to say were *also* terrible. Madison was part of a poetry/debate club in college, and his work was so bad that he was the laughingstock of the nerd club. When he heard his work read out loud, he was so embarrassed that he vowed never to be a part of something like that again. Picture that: a five-foot-four-inch thin-voiced wuss who was the least cool member of his *college poetry club.* That is not the portrait of a future president. "A Poem Against the Tories," one of three Madison poems that actually survived, ends with Madison calling his debate opponents smelly. *That was his closer.* This is supposed to be one of the brightest thinkers in history, and "you stink" is the most potent weapon in his insult arsenal?

That said, calling his mean opponents smelly was maybe the only thing Madison did wrong while in college. When he wasn't wasting his time in strange slam-poetry/word-fighting clubs, Madison was only getting four hours of sleep every night. Not because, like most college students, he wanted to party and eat too much; he simply wanted to get two years of work done in a single year so he could graduate earlier. And he did it. *While at Princeton.*

Madison worked hard on his brain to make up for his small size, but while he may have been tiny, he was still *fierce,* like Napoleon, or a goblin. Despite his height, or perhaps because of it, Madison exercised regularly to make sure that his itty-bitty frame could pack a punch. Unfortunately, he also suffered from epilepsy and arthritis, and there's no amount of exercising one can do to overcome that. One historian said he had the "frail and discernibly fragile appearance of a career librarian or a schoolmaster, forever lingering on the edge of some fatal ailment." Doesn't sound like much of a fighter.

All of Madison's mental gymnastics finally paid off. Years after he'd graduated college, when Madison was called to debate political heavyweights like Patrick Henry (considered America's greatest orator) and James Monroe (another guy, who happened to become the next president), he stepped into the ring and debated circles around them. He squared off against Monroe, a much more experienced debater, outside in the middle of a snowstorm, got frostbite, and still won!

Madison defied expectations. As long as poetry wasn't involved, Madison could convince anyone of anything. He was the one who shaped our Constitution, who wrote the Bill of Rights, and who wrote many of the Federalist Papers, successfully convincing the rest of America that the Constitution was worth ratifying. The tiny, whispery, least cool member of the nerd and poetry club was so bright and *so* persuasive that he eventually talked his way into the presidency.

Before all that, Madison managed to talk his way into the heart of Dolley Payne Todd. He did such a good job of courting her that she agreed to marry him even though they came from different religious backgrounds—a move that got her expelled from her family's Quaker church. (I told you the man could be convincing when he wanted to be.) Marrying Dolley was one of Madison's best decisions. She was charming, lively, intelligent, and the perfect hostess. Martha Washington and Abigail Adams had a good rapport with congressmen and visiting dignitaries, but Dolley was a natural hostess and turned the White House into the social center of Washington, D.C. She opened the White House up to the public and met with people from every walk of life (all of whom adored her). And if you thought James Madison was a skilled negotiator, you should know that at the very first inaugural ball, Dolley convinced both the French minister and the English minister to sit next to her at dinner, *even though their countries were at war with each other.* Dolley didn't care about that war; she thought you should use your own time to go to war, but when you're in *her* house, you abide by *her* rules.

Madison was, in his heart, a pacifist. He always believed that arguments should be settled with diplomacy instead of guns. But in 1812, as president, he felt that war was necessary. America had the right to trade at sea with any country they wanted. Great Britain refused to respect this right and tried to reduce the amount of trade between America and France, because Great Britain saw America as a threat to its naval supremacy, and because Great Britain is just such a baby sometimes. Madison tried reasoning with the British, he tried resolving things peacefully, and he tried asking the British politely to please just stop blowing up all our ships. But they wouldn't budge. Even *Napoleon* thought it was a reasonable request (great tiny minds think alike), but Great Britain held out. So, having exhausted all the peaceful options, President Madison declared war.

Two years later, that war came right to the White House. Even though he'd never fired a gun before, Madison picked up two borrowed pistols, hopped onto a horse, and rode out to the front lines. He had no previous military experience and was probably the most antiwar president we've ever had, but that didn't stop him from being the only man in history to take up arms and stand on the battlefield while being the president of the United States. Ulysses S. Grant didn't do that.

Teddy Roosevelt didn't do that. But President Madison knew how to rise to a challenge (as much as standing on your tippy-toes can be considered rising), even when all the odds were against him.

This war, called Mr. Madison's War by his critics and the Second War of Independence by the people who actually fought it, was the end of America's economic dependence on Great Britain. The first war, Madison maintained, was the Revolutionary War, while the War of 1812 was the War for Independence. Sure, this was the war that saw the burning of the White House, but it was also the war that gave us true independence *and* "The Star Spangled Banner," and it was won on James Madison's watch. (And while the White House burned, it was Madison's wife who ran in to rescue the famous portrait of George Washington, because *she was good at everything.*) Tiny, fun-sized, peace-loving James Madison overcame absolutely every single one of his many physical limitations and defied everyone's expectations, time and time again.

OFFICIAL FANTASY DREAM TEAM RATING

Madison would be a great choice for your **Brains,** but not much else. His mind is great and his passion is clear and undeniable, but he's also a tiny, sickly fella. You'd be MUCH better off recruiting Dolley, to be completely honest. She is *tough.* Unless you needed, like, a mascot or something.

5

JAMES MONROE

MADE US BIGGER AND
(IT GOES WITHOUT SAYING) BETTER!

Presidential Term: 1817–1825

Political Party: Democratic-Republican

Spouse: Elizabeth Kortright

Children: Eliza, James, and Maria

Birthdate: April 28, 1758

Death Date: July 4, 1831

Fun Fact: Monroe *also* died on the Fourth of July
(like Thomas Jefferson and John Adams).

It's unfortunate that James Monroe doesn't often get the kind of cool street cred that guys like Washington and Andrew Jackson get, because he was so tough and impressive in the Revolutionary War that British ghosts are STILL afraid to haunt his hometown. Monroe was in college at the start of the war, but that didn't stop him from rounding up twenty-four other angry patriots and breaking into the Governor's Palace in Williamsburg. Weapons and ammunition were in short supply in Virginia, so Monroe took his men and raided the palace, stealing all the decorative guns and swords off the walls and giving them to the Williamsburg militia. Liberating two hundred guns and three hundred swords and driving the royal governor away for good wasn't enough for Monroe, so he dropped out of school and joined the fight. He never went back to school, which would have been a huge disappointment to his parents had he not chosen president as his fallback career.

Monroe was an officer in the Battle of Trenton under Captain William Washington (a distant relative of George, but in NO WAY as cool). Washington, with

Monroe at his side, led the charge on the British camp, and both men were shot. Washington went down (like most people), but Monroe just thought, *Take as much time as you need, guy, I'll be captain now,* and didn't let a bullet in his shoulder get in the way of commanding his troops. It was in this battle that Monroe managed to capture two *cannons,* because he'd gotten a taste of stealing guns from people back in college and took a real liking to it. In that famous painting of George Washington crossing the Delaware, Monroe is waving the flag with the noble ferocity of a man clearly wondering if he can spin it fast enough to turn it into a propeller so that he can fly into battle.

Monroe took a few months off to recover from his bullet wound (the doctor at the time treated it by just sticking his finger in the hole for a while, because *why not,* right?), and he went back to fighting as quickly as he could, getting promotion after promotion every step of the way. Monroe did so well in the military that he was eventually promoted to a high-profile desk job that saw very little action. Most soldiers *love* the part of the war when they're not getting shot at, but Monroe got restless, quit, and went back to Virginia to try to *start his own militia.* That's like if the star quarterback left the winning team in the fourth quarter of the play-offs, started a new team, and used it to try to win the Super Bowl. But Thomas Jefferson took Monroe on as a legal apprentice before his militia could really get going, so he left military service, beloved by his men and respected by George "The Only Washington Who Really Counts" Washington.

Even though he never got a college degree, Monroe served as ambassador to France and governor of Virginia and, bizarrely, secretary of state and secretary of war *at the same time.* He was secretary of state under President Madison, who made him secretary of war when the War of 1812 broke out. Monroe resigned his old job, but no one took over, so he just thought, *UGH, fine, I'll do both.* So, he was basically advising the president on negotiating peacefully with foreign countries and their leaders as secretary of state while planning and implementing battle strategies as secretary of war. Finally, America won the war and a peace treaty was signed, and Monroe resigned as secretary of war and went back to having just one incredibly difficult job.

Monroe continued his streak of awesomeness into the presidency. For starters, he delivered a speech that was written by John Quincy Adams, which Monroe named the Monroe Doctrine, because that's one of the things you get to do when you're president. The Monroe Doctrine basically said, "Dear Europe, stay the heck away from me and stop touching my stuff. If I see your faces around North or South America, I will come at you with everything I've got. God bless America, these colors don't run, land of the free and home of the brave, USA, USA, USA!" Monroe explained that any European presence in his hemisphere would be viewed as an act of war, and at that point America had a pretty good track record for going to war with Great Britain, so Great Britain took Monroe's "get off my lawn" speech to heart and stayed away.

Even though Adams wrote the speech, it was a perfect fit for Monroe, who refused to be pushed around or intimidated his entire life. At one point during his

presidency, he had a dinner for visiting foreign diplomats. One of them somehow offended the other, so they rushed off to another room to lift their swords and duel. Monroe—as president—grabbed his own sword and joined them. He took up arms and yelled at them until they worked out their differences and went home, because they were guests in HIS house, and if you're going to wave swords around in Monroe's house, you'd better make sure Monroe's allowed to play.

A few months later, Monroe's secretary of the treasury, William Crawford, barged into Monroe's office and demanded high-ranking jobs for his buddies. President Monroe asked for time to think it over. Crawford got mad and refused to leave the office until Monroe agreed. Instead, Monroe decided to flip out, grab a set of fireplace tongs, and shout, "You will now leave the room or you will be thrust out." It's not clear what he would have *done* with those tongs, but the fact that he grabbed them must mean that he had *some* kind of plan, and this author is too terrified to even speculate.

Great Britain's decision to get off America's back also gave Monroe an opportunity to help America grow. To paraphrase, Monroe likely thought, *Truly, America is a majestic and inspiring thing of beauty, and yet I cannot help but feel like we can have EVEN MORE America.* So he acquired Florida for America, completing our run of the Eastern Shore.

OFFICIAL FANTASY DREAM TEAM RATING

Monroe was tough, which is clear from his skills on the battlefield, and he even lived his whole life with a bullet in his shoulder, which makes him a pretty strong candidate for your **Brawn** position. There are, however, much tougher presidents, and don't worry, we'll get to them.

THE PRESIDENTIAL ★ SCORECARD

? Brains
? Brawn
? Loose Cannon
? Moral Compass
? Roosevelt...

6

JOHN QUINCY ADAMS

IS ANGRY, CRAZY, AND NAKED

Presidential Term: 1825–1829
Political Party: Democratic-Republican
Spouse: Louisa Johnson
Children: Louisa, George Washington, John, and Charles Francis
Birthdate: July 11, 1767
Death Date: February 23, 1848
Fun Fact: Adams had a pet alligator, because the
1800s were *so much cooler than the present.*

At the age of eight, John Quincy Adams was made the man of the house while his father, John Adams, was off doing important John Adams things for America. This would be a lot of terrifying responsibility at any time in American history, but it just so happens that when Adams was eight years old, the American Revolution was happening right outside his house. The house he had sworn to protect. He watched the Battle of Bunker Hill from his front porch, according to his diary, worried that he might be "butchered in cold blood, or taken and carried . . . as hostages by any foraging or marauding detachment" of British soldiers. I don't have the diary I kept at age eight, but I think the only things I worried about were whether they'd have corn dogs for lunch in school the next day and if I would be able to collect all the Pokémon. John Quincy, on the other hand, guarded his house, mother, and siblings during wartime.

This experience—coupled with the fact that his father was John "I'm the President So If You Grow Up to Be Anything Else, It Will Be Viewed as a Tremendous Disappointment" Adams (presidential nicknames can't all be as catchy as Old Hickory)—inspired John Quincy's intense drive, sense of duty, and unstoppable quest for perfection in the pursuit of serving his country and pleasing his father. He was the private secretary and interpreter to the U.S. minister to Russia at fourteen and secretary at the Treaty of Paris at sixteen. He has held more diplomatic posts than any other American politician and is the only president who served in Congress *after* his presidency. Most presidents don't *need* to take a job after they leave office because they figure, *You know what? I was president. I'm probably not gonna top that.* But John Q. thought, *Okay, I've done four years in that job. What else can I do to help the world?* Because John Quincy is better than us.

As he got older, Adams only got *tougher* (he exercised regularly, swimming the width of the Potomac River at five a.m. every single day, even as a fifty-eight-year-old president), *more intelligent* (his skills as a diplomat are legendary), and *more naked* (he exercised, swam, and took walks in the nude).

He also kept an alligator as a pet, right in the White House. That has nothing to do with his policies or anything, it just seems like it's worth bringing up. Name a cooler White House pet, right now. See? You can't. Until they bring dinosaurs back, you can't.

Because of his father's accomplishments, John Quincy was never satisfied. At sixty-five, he wrote in his diary that his "whole life [had] been a succession of disappointment. I scarcely recollect a single instance of success to anything that I ever undertook."

"What about that time you were president?" his diary would have asked, if diaries were capable of asking questions in the 1800s, but John Quincy wouldn't have listened no matter *what* his diary said because his inability to live up to the ridiculous expectations he set for himself drove him to depression, self-loathing, and intense self-punishment. He wrote most of the Monroe Doctrine and was instrumental in negotiating the treaty that ended the War of 1812, but he still never believed he was doing enough. The physical exercises he did every day (for anywhere between two and five hours) had nothing to do with staying in *shape;* he was tor-

turing himself for not being perfect. If he wasn't punishing himself with sprinting or swimming against the Potomac's current, he would soak for hours in an ice-cold bath and rub his body down with a horsehair mitten, something that *sounds* adorable but is super painful. It was torture. John Quincy would engage in this intense level of self-punishment as *president*.

It wasn't just his own body that John Quincy liked punishing; it was also his opponents. The only thing that gave him an emotional high more powerful than the one he got by beating himself up was beating up his opponents, especially if he could single-handedly fight *multiple* opponents. His ego was fueled by victory and self-righteousness, and as time went on, he came to be feared in Congress for his ferocity, persistence, and habit of outshouting the chairman whenever he tried

to tell him he was out of order (probably for shouting too loud). John Quincy spent every day believing that it was just him against the world, and he *loved* this feeling.

He was also a little mentally imbalanced, in case that isn't clear by now. Apparently so much of his brain was devoted to making peace around the world while fighting endless little battles closer to home that there was no room left in that giant skull of his for the part of the brain that's supposed to focus on reason and rationality. While president (of, it should be stressed, the whole country), Adams was approached by a man named John Cleves Symmes Jr., who fervently believed that the Earth was hollow and full of tiny civilizations. He even drew a map of a hollow Earth with a bunch of busy little civilizations made up of mole people to drive his point home. *"There are mole people living beneath us,"* Symmes stressed.

Then John Quincy Adams *agreed with him.* He thought it was visionary and considered it his great fortune that *he personally* could help kick off this expedition and maybe open up trade relations *with the mole people.*

John Quincy Adams, a man smart enough to read and put on pants (when he felt like it), saw a map about a hollow Earth full of mole people and thought, *Hey, I bet we can trade with those mole people! What do moles like? Sugar? Hats? You know what, it doesn't matter. Take a bunch of the taxpayers' money, go to the North Pole, and start digging.* There's no exaggeration here. That was his actual plan.

Thankfully, Adams left office before he could actually see this plan through. He lost his reelection bid to Andrew Jackson, who had spent four years rigorously campaigning. When Andrew Jackson stepped into the presidency, he shut the project down, because even he could see that the plan fell somewhere between arguing with cats and eating your own poop on the spectrum of stupid ideas. The plan was too insane for *Andrew Jackson,* and he was so nuts that—Well, you'll see, I don't want to spoil it.

As we know, Adams continued to serve his country in Congress, postpresidency. Fittingly, he fought and worked for his country right up until he was hit with a massive cerebral hemorrhage literally in the middle of answering a question in the House of Representatives. He was halfway through replying to a question from the Speaker of the House when his brain, disappointed that all the *other* brains get time off occasionally, just gave up and said, *"Nope. We're done here."*

OFFICIAL FANTASY DREAM TEAM RATING

His mind is great and his dedication is impressive, but come on, he thought the Earth was hollow and full of mole people. You're building an elite team—there's no room for the guy who might FLIP OUT at any time.

7

ANDREW JACKSON

THE MAN FEARED BY GUNS

Presidential Term: 1829–1837
Political Party: Democratic
Spouse: Rachel Donelson
Children: Theodore, Andrew Jr., and Lyncoya (all adopted)
Birthdate: March 15, 1767
Death Date: June 8, 1845
Fun Fact: The celebratory party following his inauguration was SO INSANE that Jackson needed to jump out a window of the White House to go somewhere private and get some actual work done.

Andrew Jackson, the wild-eyed, hard-fighting, hard-partying, cane-wielding, enemy-stomping son of a gun who ran our country for eight years, was a whole lot of things, and all of them were crazy. He wasn't always a lunatic, of course; he *aged* into it, like a fine wine, fermented with poison and stirred with an ax. If "violence and hatred" were a drink, it would never leave Jackson's flask, but since it's *not* a drink, he drank whiskey instead to fuel his rage. According to historians, Jackson would hate with a "grand passion" and would "resort to petty and vindictive acts to nurture his hatred and keep it bright and strong and ferocious," much like the man himself. In fact, I'm terrified just writing this chapter.

Jackson's bad attitude and paranoia started when he was very young. Jackson was born without a father and his mother died when he was fourteen. As a result, he expected death to be lurking around every corner and was prepared to fight at any moment, which he did, all throughout school. Often picked on by bullies,

Jackson would frequently come home with bruises, scars, and scrapes. At thirteen years old, having bested every available schoolyard bully in a three-state radius, Jackson decided to fight the British in the Revolutionary War, which is more impressive than probably anything that any thirteen-year-old has done in the last one hundred years. A thirteen-year-old would need to do a backflip *while curing cancer* to be cooler than Jackson.

In 1780, thirteen-year-old Jackson was captured by British soldiers and taken as a prisoner of war, along with his brother Robert. There he was ordered to shine his enemies' shoes, and his refusal earned him a long gash down his cheek. He was then forced to march wounded and shoeless, without food or water and full of bright and shiny hatred, for forty miles from one prison camp to another, all while suffering from smallpox. The smallpox killed his brother but was just terrified enough of Jackson to back off quietly. He fought in a war, got stabbed in the face, marched miles barefoot, lost his brother, and beat smallpox—and that's just his teen years!

Even with all he suffered during the Revolutionary War, a fearless Jackson went on to fight in the War of 1812 and the First Seminole War, and when he ran out of wars, he just went duel crazy. Jackson was in thirteen duels *that we know of.* While some historians dispute this number, everyone agrees that he loved a duel.

One duel in particular stands out among all the rest. In 1806, Jackson challenged Charles Dickinson to a duel over gambling debts. Though Dickinson was widely known as a good shot, Jackson allowed him to fire first. It would be irresponsible of me not to repeat that: in a duel with pistols, Jackson *politely volunteered to be shot first.* Dickinson fired, nailed Jackson almost in the heart, and started to reload. Before he could finish, Jackson shot him dead. The man plays punch for punch with *bullets.* He recovered from his wound (he, in fact, had the good sense to immediately put his hand over it, while still dueling, to stanch the bleeding) but lived with chronic pain for the rest of his life.

Jackson *lived* to duel, and you know there's only one way you can survive multiple duels: you're really, *really* good at them. Losing a duel isn't like losing at soccer (unless your soccer league is really hard-core); you get shot and then you die. Between his dueling and his military career, Jackson had been shot so many times that scholars say he "rattled like a bag of marbles" when he walked as a result of all the bullets left in his body.

Of course, Jackson wasn't just lethal with a gun; he was also pretty handy with his trademark hickory cane. In 1835, a lunatic named Richard Lawrence made the first documented assassination attempt on a president's life when he pulled a gun on Andrew Jackson. The gun misfired, so he pulled out a second gun, *which also misfired.* Upon later inspection, both guns fired without error. Some historians

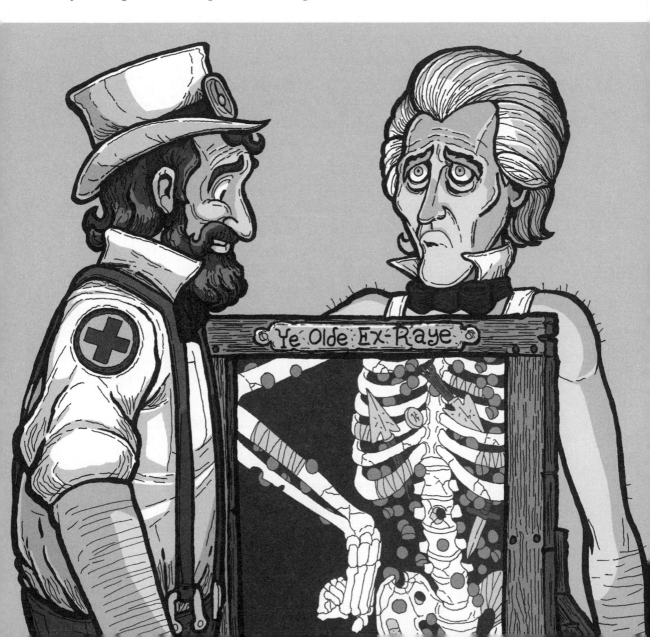

blamed the weather for the temporary misfiring, but it's pretty clear that the bullets, having previously consulted the *other* bullets rattling around Jackson's body, had no interest in getting involved with such a futile suicide mission, since every bullet knows that Jackson doesn't believe in getting shot to death. After Jackson got tired of watching Lawrence pull out gun after terrified gun, he beat Lawrence with his cane until presidential aides had to restrain *Jackson*.

Jackson's not just tough by presidential standards. He's not just tough by *human* standards. He stacks up against the Terminator and Liam Neeson; the man is tough by *movie hero standards*. Do you want Jackson on your Presidential Fantasy Dream Team? Of course you do, if only because you should be terrified NOT to ask for his help.

Here is what you need to know about Andrew Jackson: he is a man followed by tragedy. He lost friends, family members, and his beloved wife, Rachel. Rachel was a lovely woman, but she was very frail and anxious. She wanted a quiet life on a farm, but Jackson had political dreams, and even though it made her nervous, she supported him. Unfortunately, the strain of being a future president's wife ended up being too much for her; when Jackson was campaigning, his opponents tried to spread rumors about Rachel. She was still technically married to her previous husband when she married Jackson, but that was only the result of a silly technical error, which was easily corrected. His opponents didn't care. They took this small technical error and ran with it, painting Rachel as an improper woman who was juggling multiple husbands. When Rachel learned of these attacks (posted in leaflets and newspapers), the distress combined with the stress of campaigning proved to be too much for her, and she died of a heart attack shortly before Jackson took office. Jackson loved her so much that he needed to be pulled from her body so the undertaker could prepare her.

Andrew never remarried after Rachel died, so America became his replacement family. And this was one family Andrew Jackson was determined not to lose. He loved, lived for, and worshipped America. It completed him. Jackson saw himself as both the physical embodiment of America and its sworn protector. An attack on Jackson meant an attack on America, and if he thought someone wanted to hurt America, you'd better believe he'd react like a crazed father protecting his children.

Despite a legacy consisting of enough violence and death for twenty men, Jackson admitted to having two deathbed regrets: "I didn't shoot Henry Clay and I didn't hang John C. Calhoun." In a life full of wars and duels, Jackson's only regret was that he *didn't kill quite enough people*. People like Calhoun, who, it should be noted, was Jackson's vice president.

OFFICIAL FANTASY DREAM TEAM RATING

Oh my God, yes, you'd be smart to want him on *your* side. Every great super squad needs a crazy **Loose Cannon.**

★ 8

MARTIN VAN BUREN

PRESIDENT KING

Presidential Term: 1837–1841
Political Party: Democratic
Spouse: Hannah Hoes
Children: Abraham, John, Martin Jr., Winfield, and Smith
Birthdate: December 5, 1782
Death Date: July 24, 1862
Fun Fact: Every previous president was technically born a British citizen, making Van Buren our first American-born president.

Martin Van Buren was a crummy guy. Not just because he was a bad president (though, yes, he was), and not just because he was pro-slavery. Van Buren was crummy in a very general sort of way, and with all that that implies. If you were related to him, you'd dread Thanksgiving every year because you'd know *he* would be there, with his stupid stories and overbearing crumminess. If you saw him walking toward you, you'd cross to the other side of the street, out of fear that his aggressive and practiced crumminess would rub off on you. If you two went to high school together, you wouldn't be friends with him.

It is my personal and admittedly ridiculous theory that Van Buren's schoolmasters are solely responsible for his crumminess. Looking at Van Buren's handwriting, and reading accounts about the man from people who knew him, I find that all signs point to him most likely being born left-handed. His schoolmasters, perhaps worried that Van Buren was a witch, would regularly beat him in the hand with a cane until he learned to write with his right hand. This lesson says it all about Van Buren, because it forced him to act in a way that contradicted what was right. Writing with his left hand felt right, but he had been conditioned to do the *opposite* of right (which, yes, troublingly in this case means using his right hand). As a result of this conditioning, from that moment on, Van Buren was determined to do what was wrong at every pass. Or, for the purposes of this chapter, what was *crummy*.

Early in his political career, Van Buren figured out how to exploit the game of politics. America was entering a political period in which the *people* were really starting to shine, to step up and elect the candidates *they* wanted—showing that power really *does* come from the people. Van Buren took a look at that promise and thought, *Oh, hey, I totally know how to cheat that.* Known as the Little Magician or the Red Fox for his ability to manipulate and mastermind elections (like foxes?), Van Buren formed the Albany Regency in 1822. The Albany Regency was what was called a political machine—a group of slimy politicians who basically controlled all of New York state government for over a decade. They didn't control the government by being *elected* into power by the *people* in 1822; they got together to rig New York elections and place their friends and relatives in important positions of power. And Van Buren was their leader.

Since Van Buren understood how to game the political system as well as he did, it was no surprise that he would eventually become president. I should be clear: Martin Van Buren didn't want to be a *good* president; he just wanted to *be* president, and enjoy himself while doing it. He wanted the attention, he wanted the power, he wanted the status, and that was it. There was only one issue about which he was passionate, and that was his stance on slavery (pro!). In his inaugural address, Van Buren said, "I must go into the presidential chair the inflexible and uncompromising opponent of every attempt on the part of Congress to abolish slavery in the District of Columbia," an appropriate prelude to the presidency of crumminess that would soon follow.

When not fighting Congress on slavery, Van Buren spent his time in the White House throwing fancy parties for his fancy friends and spending lots of money on furniture. As an ambassador to Great Britain (you know, that place America worked so hard to distance itself from), he fell in love with the parties and royal lifestyle (you know, that thing America worked so hard to make sure never corrupted its democracy), and his autobiography is just page after page of name-dropping from this period. He wanted everyone to know how many famous royal people he met in England, and how many cool parties he'd been invited to.

Martin Van Buren loved the fanciness and respectability of British royalty so much that he tried to bring it back with him to America. He spent a fortune redecorating the White House ($27,000 of which came from the American taxpayer, which would be just shy of $540,000 in today's dollars) to make it a more appropriate

home for the kind of aristocrat Van Buren wanted to be. Jackson was the people's president, a man who invited the entire nation to party with him to celebrate his presidency. Van Buren, on the other hand, turned the White House into a palace, with policemen stationed outside to make sure no "improper" people ever entered. (There was no Secret Service yet.) He dressed like a big, snooty Mr. Fancy-Pants who thinks he's too good for us too. Davy Crockett, a guy entirely composed of iron and manliness, described Van Buren as a "dandy" who would walk around "laced up in corsets, such as women . . . wear. It would be difficult to say, from his personal appearance, whether he was a man or woman."

Van Buren lived lavishly and spent all this money, by the way, during the Panic of 1837, the most devastating economic collapse in American history (until the Great Depression almost one hundred years later). Everyone was out of work, struggling, and helpless while Van Buren was sipping wine, flaunting his resources, and enjoying the most relaxing presidency ever. His critics dubbed him Martin Van Ruin, which I brought up only to let everyone reading this know that I intend to use that as my own nickname, should I ever decide to enter professional wrestling.

Van Buren didn't care that everyone was trashing his name or that the country was falling apart on his watch, because he didn't have any strong opinions at all. He avoided controversial subjects, and whenever he was asked his opinion on literally anything, he would dress up his answer in so much vague language and double-talk that no one ever knew where he stood on any issue.

Van Buren, rightly and obviously, did not win a second term. He tried running twice more as a third-party candidate when his *own* Democratic Party refused to nominate him, but mostly he enjoyed his retirement in an alarmingly, though completely characteristically, crummy way. He sometimes gambled, but not at a casino or with friends; falling back on the lessons he picked up in his Albany Regency days, he would gamble on elections that he personally rigged. Rigging elections wasn't crummy enough for Van Buren; he needed to profit from them and dress it up as a lucky gambling win.

OFFICIAL FANTASY DREAM TEAM RATING

Van Buren does not belong on your Fantasy Dream Team, and if any of your friends *do* support Van Buren, I'd turn and run the other way and seriously reevaluate the way you choose friends.

THE PRESIDENTIAL ★ SCORECARD

? Brains
? Brawn
? Loose Cannon
? Moral Compass
? Roosevelt...

9

WILLIAM HENRY HARRISON

COULD HAVE CHANGED HISTORY IF HE'D WORN A COAT

Presidential Term: 1841
Political Party: Whig
Spouse: Anna Symmes
Children: Elizabeth, John, Lucy, William Jr., John Scott, Benjamin, Mary, Carter, Anna, and James (Wow! That's so many children.)
Birthdate: February 9, 1773
Death Date: April 4, 1841
Fun Fact: Harrison's wife was related to the guy who thought the Earth was hollow and full of mole people (see the John Quincy Adams chapter).

William Henry Harrison was one of those rare men who only had two main jobs in his life: soldier and president. A child of the Revolutionary War (when he was eight, Harrison's home was attacked by Hessian troops, which contrasts starkly with the cartoon watching that you likely did at that age), Harrison joined the army in 1791. Well, actually, he briefly studied medicine first, but he decided that taking lives was much more exciting than saving them. And it all worked out, because as history shows, William Henry Harrison was *great* at taking lives.

Harrison fought in the Indian Wars for a while, earning the admiration of presidents Madison, Jefferson, and John "Not Quincy" Adams (and precisely no Native Americans). He toyed with leaving the military behind for politics, but even as a governor of the Indiana Territory, he was still fighting battles and leading attacks against Tecumseh and his Native American forces. In 1811, Tecumseh and his troops snuck up on Governor Harrison and his troops near Tippecanoe, and even though it was early in the morning and Tecumseh's men had the element of surprise on their side (Harrison's men were asleep when the Native Americans attacked), Harrison woke up and, in two hours, drove the Native Americans away and burned their camp to the ground, effectively stopping any future Native American intervention in their territory. This earned Harrison the nickname Old Tippecanoe, because, seriously, the guys who handed out nicknames did not have their acts together for a very long time. Harrison led this charge and personally fought in hand-to-hand combat as *governor,* which, on paper, is supposed to be one of the least-fightingest jobs one could have (next to, perhaps, "Professional Presidential Fantasy Dream Team Historian"). Harrison then quit being governor and rejoined the army for the War of 1812, because even though he was fighting in more battles than any other governor, he *still* wasn't satisfied by the amount of fighting in his life.

Harrison was a man for whom fighting and battle were everything. He met his future wife, Anna Symmes, while on military business, and when her father (a prominent judge) disapproved of Anna's hasty marriage to him, Harrison dealt with the man the only way he knew how—as a soldier. When Symmes demanded to know how Harrison would support his daughter, Harrison immediately replied, "By my sword, sir, and my good right arm." Some guys ask the girl's father for permission to marry his daughter, but William Henry Harrison waves a sword around at a judge. And it worked. Harrison got to keep Anna *and* won her father's approval.

After he had stabbed his way into a marriage, Harrison went right back to fighting the War of 1812, which involved taking back Indiana, Ohio, and Detroit from British and Native American forces and winning a decisive victory at the Battle of the Thames (the battle where Tecumseh, the feared Shawnee Native American leader, was finally killed). He was a national hero, but he left the army over a disagreement with the secretary of war; Harrison wanted command of the *whole* army, and the secretary thought it would be best to divide the army up and just give Harrison *some* of it. Harrison apparently had plans that he simply couldn't act on without an entire army under his command, so he resigned. Congress would later investigate Harrison's resignation, conclude that he was treated unfairly, and award him a gold medal. Once more: the man got a gold war medal for *quitting*.

Maybe it was because he still wanted to be in charge of the army without having to answer to any pesky secretary of war, but whatever the reason, as soon as Harrison retired from military service, he sought the presidency. William Henry Harrison wasn't like a lot of other war-heroes-turned-presidents. Most of those men (like Ulysses S. Grant or Zachary Taylor), just sort of stumbled into the presidency on the strength of their national popularity. Harrison *wanted* the presidency, and he was just sneaky enough that he didn't really care how he got it. In 1840, after trying and failing twice in his pursuit of the office, Harrison was prepared to lie.

The Whig Party wanted some way to distance their candidate, Harrison, from the incumbent Van Buren, so they turned Harrison into a folksy blue-collar hero, earning him the label of the Log Cabin and Hard Cider candidate. Harrison campaigned all over the country for years, reassuring everyone the whole time that he was a fun-loving guy you could sit down and have a beer with. But it wasn't enough for Harrison to be *just* the cool good old boy; he also needed to make Van Buren look like an elitist aristocrat.

Harrison and his team started releasing flyers with illustrations of Harrison next to a log cabin to demonstrate his down-to-earth authenticity and prove conclusively that he could be physically near a log cabin (in a drawing, anyway). The Whigs threw parades full of log cabin floats, folks drank whiskey out of log cabin–shaped flasks to show support (somehow), and America ate it up. In a time when political machines were running things and it seemed like only an elite few made it into Washington, it was nice to see Harrison—a decent down-home guy—seeking office.

Here's the thing: Harrison was about as down-home and folksy as a cold Terminator robot sent back in time to be a crappy president. Harrison *didn't* live in a log cabin *or* drink hard cider. He had acres and acres of land surrounding his mansion in Ohio, where he fought as a prohibitionist to close alcohol distilleries. Van Buren might have been an elitist, but as a guy who was born and raised in a tavern, he certainly had a better claim to the "Log Cabin and Hard Cider" label than Harrison.

In light of today's political campaigns, in which *every* candidate has an image that's carefully constructed and maintained by a dedicated PR team, this might not seem like a huge deal, but it was fairly revolutionary at the time. Harrison's entire campaign was based around selling an image, not a person. Harrison didn't actually run on any issues. His campaign manager actually said, "Let no committee, no convention, no town meeting extract from him a single word about what he thinks now or what he will do hereafter." Harrison went along with it, because he wanted the presidency. He wanted it badly enough that he didn't care about his reputation, and he certainly wasn't above rubbing dirt all over Van Buren's crummy name. Harrison's team even started an ugly rumor that Van Buren installed a *bathtub* in the *White House* (apparently in the 1840s only jerks bathed), and the public went nuts. Can you believe that? A bathtub. Like *some kind of useless idiot jerk.*

The campaign worked (and this lesson was adopted by every campaign that followed). Seventy-eight percent of the voters chose Harrison, because they fell

for the lie about how real he was. Harrison, the uncompromising war hero, let his ambition blind him to anything else and lied his way into the White House.

So, now Harrison is the president. Was he going to play up his "log cabin" status and serve as a man of the people, or would he play to his true nature and serve the behind-the-scenes people who actually made him president? Well, we'll never know. On Harrison's inauguration day, the weather was terrible. Still, he gave his inaugural address outside during a freezing rainstorm, without an overcoat or a hat or gloves or anything else that might have kept him warm. Maybe he was trying to show off how tough he was, or maybe he was still trying to play up his realness because overcoats are for fancy people and Harrison was a *man's* man. We'll never know. But we do know that he delivered a two-hour speech in the cold, got sick, and died after being president for only a month. Now the only thing Harrison's presidency is remembered for is its brevity.

OFFICIAL FANTASY DREAM TEAM RATING

Um . . . he died thirty-two days after being inaugurated after lying his way into office, so . . . no.

10

JOHN TYLER

AMERICA'S ACCIDENT

Presidential Term: 1841–1845
Political Party: Whig and Democratic
Spouses: Letitia Christian and Julia Gardiner
Children: Mary, Robert, John, Letitia, Elizabeth, Anne, Alice, and Tazewell
with his wife Letitia; and David, John Alexander, Julia, Lachlan, Lyon, Robert Fitzwalter,
and Pearl with his wife Julia—giving him more
children than any other president
Birthdate: March 29, 1790
Death Date: January 18, 1862
Fun Fact: Tyler was the first president no one elected!

John Tyler was born to be a rebel. No one knows what started it, but rejecting authority and taking matters into his own hands was simply in Tyler's blood. In elementary school, Tyler disagreed with the headmaster of his school, which is standard, so he organized his fellow classmates and staged a *revolt*, which is *crazy*. Sure, we all *thought* about it, but Tyler *did* it, because he is a *loose cannon*, and while most kids grow out of their youthful rebellion phase, Tyler let it define him.

Tyler was always fighting with whoever the authority was, even if the authority was the president, and even if the president was Andrew Jackson. Tyler made a name for himself as a senator by repeatedly criticizing President Jackson, voting against almost every nomination Jackson proposed. Tyler did this despite being a member of the same party as Jackson, and in fact, Tyler's vocal condemnations of Jackson were considered an act of insurgency by his party. Tyler was originally a Democrat like Jackson, and he stayed that way until, like a good little rebel, he got fed up, quit, and joined a new party: the Whigs. He rose up the ranks of the Whig Party quickly and was grateful when they made him William Henry Harrison's running mate. It's possible that Tyler would have fought with Harrison, as he fought with every authority figure in his life, but we'll never know for sure, since Harrison died before anyone had a chance to decide if he was a good president.

John Tyler was the first man to serve as president without being elected. In modern times, we all understand that the vice president is the person who is supposed to step in when the president dies, but remember that this idea didn't *always* exist. Vice presidents were elected to balance the president, not to be *future* presidents in case the actual president died. Tyler stepped in when Harrison died, setting a president precedent and earning himself the unfortunate, but appropriate, nickname His Accidency. This was actually a fairly inspired move; most people assumed a new election would be held, and some thought Tyler should just be an "acting president" until Congress decided what to do, but Tyler didn't give them the chance. No one had the opportunity to sit around discussing what to do next, because shortly after Harrison died, Tyler put his hand on the Bible, took the oath of office, and essentially flat out *told* everyone, *"Hey, I'm the president now. Deal with it."* He promptly proceeded to tell Harrison's cabinet that regardless of how they did things under Harrison, *Tyler* was in charge now. They were going to listen to him, and if anyone didn't like it they could leave, because *nobody* tells Tyler what to do. That's a pretty impressive move for someone who had no clear or legal right to be so impressive.

Tyler's first order of business as president was to tick off absolutely everyone. Whig leader Henry Clay expected Tyler to work closely with the Whigs (as Harrison would have done). But even *that* felt too much like manipulation to Tyler. Tyler vetoed most of Clay's proposed legislations. One by one, everyone in Tyler's cabinet resigned out of protest—and because Tyler refused to listen to anyone he thought was trying to influence or control him (which, according to Tyler, was everyone). When Tyler didn't change his policies even after his entire cabinet resigned, the Whigs officially kicked Tyler out of the party. This makes Tyler the only standing president who was dropped by his own party, and it's all because Tyler was worried that the Whigs were going to try to push him around. John Quincy Adams unsuccessfully tried to get Tyler impeached, and his critics in the media dubbed Tyler the President Without a Party, setting a precedent for James Dean and any other future rebels who would go without things. Tyler's decision to alienate his own party had a devastating impact on his presidential legacy. The Whigs voted against him at every turn, and as a result, he accomplished very little and is considered inept by most historians. He managed to officially add Texas as a state to the Union, which was certainly cool. When he realized he was losing most of his friends and support, he turned all his focus to annexing Texas. He cleared out any staffers who weren't pro-Texas and hired a bunch of people who *were*, then went on an American tour to improve his image. It worked, insofar as it convinced senators to back his plan and add Texas to the country, but it wasn't enough to ensure another term. Because of his steadfast refusal to play nice and make friends, he never had a chance of getting a second term. With no party backing him for reelection, Tyler briefly considered forming his own party, but he backed down at the last second.

In one final act of rebellion, Tyler spent his last few days in office throwing one amazing and legendary party. Tyler sent out two thousand invitations (though three thousand people eventually showed up, proving that even if the host is generally disliked, no one can turn down a free party), and "eight dozen bottles of champagne were drunk with wine by the barrels" and property was destroyed.

Tyler threw this party for no reason other than to deliver a silly little pun. When Tyler left the White House shortly thereafter, he remarked, "Yes, they cannot say now that I am *a President without a party*." Then he put on sunglasses and a wicked guitar solo just *happened*.

After his presidency, Tyler retired to his plantation, which he named Sherwood Forest. He saw himself as a Robin Hood figure, which is weird, because Robin Hood stole from the rich and gave to the poor, and John Tyler stole the presidency and owned like forty slaves. Lest you think that Tyler's rebellious streak was all fun, you should know that being a rebel *also* meant rebelling against the Union. Yes, when Tyler left office, he joined the Confederacy and turned on the nation over which he used to preside. He was considered a traitor, and he was the only former president

whose death wasn't officially announced or memorialized by the White House. He died of a stroke in 1862, three years before the Civil War ended, as a man on the wrong side of history. He took a sip of brandy and reportedly told his doctor, "I am going. Perhaps it is best."

OFFICIAL FANTASY DREAM TEAM RATING

Does it need to be said? Don't add the do-nothing president to your Fantasy Dream Team.

THE PRESIDENTIAL ★ SCORECARD

(?) Brains
(?) Brawn
(?) Loose Cannon
(?) Moral Compass
(?) Roosevelt...

11

JAMES K. POLK

A MAN WITH A PLAN

Presidential Term: 1845–1849

Political Party: Democratic

Spouse: Sarah Childress

Children: None

Birthdate: November 2, 1795

Death Date: June 15, 1849

Fun Fact: The "l" in Polk's name is silent—*but deadly.*

"Polk who?"

That's probably the question you're asking right now, as the average American probably doesn't know or care who Polk is. But that problem isn't just unique to our times; the Whig Party, Polk's opponents when he ran for president as a Democrat back in 1844, used his relative obscurity to their advantage during the campaign. They talked about his inexperience and laughed about what little impact he had made on America. No one apart from Andrew Jackson had heard of Polk.

Polk's introverted behavior and lack of popularity made him the first-ever dark-horse candidate. He received his presidential nomination solely on the strength of Andrew Jackson's endorsement; Polk worked for Jackson during Jackson's first presidential campaign, and the two became fast friends, so Jackson took a real shine to Polk. And when Andrew Jackson tells his party to do something, *they do it.* Almost everyone at the time said he was a poor choice who had no chance of winning (the *New York Herald* commented that "a more ridiculous, contemptible, and forlorn candidate was never put forth by any party"), and almost everyone *since* has completely forgotten about him.

This is a tragedy. Polk is one of the most underrated presidents ever, both in terms of his accomplishments and his position on the spectrum of coolness. He was just a little guy, and he was prone to illness as a child. While Polk may have lacked physical strength, he made up for it with his determination to not let his size hold him back in any way. Biographer Charles Sellers said that as a result of his "early physical inferiority," he "drove himself ruthlessly, exploiting the abilities and energies he did possess to an extent that few men can equal."

The most important thing you need to know about Polk is that he was a man who accomplished what he set out to do, no matter what. He is the only president who knew exactly what he wanted to do when he got to office, exactly how he would do it, and exactly how long it would take. When he took office, Polk made a list of four very lofty goals that he was going to accomplish before his time was up: (1) reestablish the independent treasury system to take government money *away* from the banks and place it in a special reserve that the government could control; (2) reduce tariffs; (3) acquire (by any means necessary) some of the Oregon Country from Great Britain; and (4) get California and New Mexico from Mexico. Polk dedicated every second of his time in office to pursuing those goals. Polk's to-do list was impressive enough for most presidents, but Polk decided to do the political equivalent of tying one hand behind his back and saying, *"Oh, and by the way, I'm going to do it all in just* one *term,"* and then dramatically dropped the microphone and walked off the stage. (He would have, had microphones been invented then. He probably just dropped a pen or fist-bumped his vice president or something instead.)

Even though this plan seems way too ambitious, a combination of Polk's passion and intensity helped him pull it off. He accomplished all his goals, and he added some bonus states by buying the Oregon Territory from the British, which included Washington, Oregon, Idaho, and parts of Montana and Wyoming. He also got us a chunk of the Southwest from Mexico, first by trying to buy it, but when Mexico said, *"Uh, we're not actually selling,"* he just straight up took it from them in the Mexican-American War (a domestic war that successfully wrapped up in one term *and that wasn't even on his list*). The states acquired by the United States in the Treaty of Guadalupe Hidalgo (the treaty ending the Mexican-American War) included California, Nevada, Utah, and Arizona, and parts of New Mexico, Colorado, and Wyoming. Polk made America bigger (which, as any scientist will tell you, means he also made it better), fulfilling America's Manifest Destiny by expanding our territory to the Western shores. And he did it in less than four years, just like he said he would. When it was time to plan for his second term, Polk looked around at his accomplishments and simply thought, *Nah, I'm good. Pretty much nailed it in one,* and chose not to seek reelection. There's not a single other president in the history of America that can boast a similar success rate.

Not only did Polk knock his presidency out of the park in one term, but he did it almost entirely by himself. Dubbed the Lone Wolf President by at least one guy who writes books about Presidential Fantasy Dream Teams, Polk had a problem trusting anyone who wasn't his wife, Sarah. Whenever he was faced with a problem, he opted to handle things himself, and that didn't change when he rose to the highest office in the land. He once said that he preferred to "supervise the whole operations of Government myself rather than entrust the public business to subordinates and this makes my duties very great." His focus and determination extended to Sarah as well, who, unlike most First Ladies before her, shared Polk's political ambitions and helped him write speeches and letters, and advised him about anything else that came across his desk. This is an all-business, no-nonsense couple we're talking about here. When he and Sarah hosted parties at the White House, they did so coldly and efficiently; alcohol (except wine for special guests), smoking, gambling, *dancing,* and anything else that could be considered a vice was not welcome in the Polks' White House, and Sarah earned the nickname Sahara Sarah for keeping the White House dry (meaning free of alcohol). Nothing was going to distract these two from running the nation; Sarah even refused to go to the *theater,* and in the 1800s that was one of the only forms of entertainment. Polk practically locked himself in the White House every single day, leaving only to go to church with Sarah. The few vacations he took only happened because Sarah *demanded* he take them out of concern for his health.

It was a good thing the Democrats controlled both the House and the Senate during Polk's administration, because who knows what would have happened if Congress tried to get in his way. Polk was simply a man who embraced the policy of doing something yourself if you want it done right, and he had Congress to back him up. Hey, it worked for him, and that's why today America is America "from sea to shining sea," and not America "from sea to wherever Mexico or Great Britain said 'stop.'"

I didn't quite give you the whole story of how Polk took America to the Pacific Coast. Polk addressed Congress and requested permission to declare war against Mexico, claiming that Mexican forces had entered American territory and "shed American blood on American soil." Congress, obviously, couldn't say no to that. War was declared, Polk sent out the troops, and before anyone had a chance to investigate, the war was over and California was ours. (In typical dry fashion, Polk announced the news by simply saying that war exists and that he had sent troops to go conquer some peace.)

Here's the thing: there's significant evidence that Mexican forces not only didn't draw first blood on American soil, but they also (a) didn't even invade American territory and (b) didn't draw first blood *at all*. A full investigation into the matter never took place, as Polk had riled the American people into such a fury at that point that anyone who tried to challenge him would be deemed unpatriotic (including Abraham Lincoln, a young and ambitious lawyer at the time).

Did Polk lie his way into this war just to make America stronger and further his agenda? We'll never know, but probably. Polk is the kind of man who can make these sorts of tough, potentially illegal decisions in the interest of serving the greater good, assuming the "greater good" is code for "whatever Polk wants."

Described even by his enemies as the hardest-working man in Washington, Polk didn't really have any hobbies or interests outside of his work. He was terrible in social situations, he didn't have any friends, and he never bothered to have any children, because he didn't want anything to stall him on the road to political greatness.

He died three months after leaving office of chronic diarrhea and, let's face it, utter humiliation at dying from chronic diarrhea. He was fifty-three years old. It was a tragic end to an incredible presidency, but also proof that Polk knew what he was doing when he chose not to try for a second term. He was put on this earth to spread America to the West Coast, and having finished the job, it was time to go. He didn't just leave the White House after his work was done; he left *life*. The man knew how to quit when he was ahead.

Sarah, on the other hand, continued to live for another forty-two years and wore black every single day to better mourn her late husband. (I told you these people were *dedicated*, right?) When the Civil War broke out, Sarah offered her home as a place for Union *and* Confederate generals to meet. It was a rare, truly neutral place of peace in the middle of a war. The Polks really knew how not to party.

OFFICIAL FANTASY DREAM TEAM RATING

You want him. No one likes to admit it, but every effective supersquad needs someone willing to get their hands dirty and bend the rules in the interest of getting stuff *done*. Polk is such a person. He's a perfect fit for your **Loose Cannon.**

His wife too. If you have an option to draft First Ladies into your team, Sarah Polk is your gal. Even if you just make her your mascot, she could still secretly work as your advisor and teammate.

12

ZACHARY TAYLOR

IS READY TO PLAY ROUGH

Presidential Term: 1849–1850
Political Party: Whig
Spouse: Margaret Smith
Children: Ann, Sarah, Octavia, Margaret, Mary, and Richard
Birthdate: November 24, 1784
Death Date: July 9, 1850
Fun Fact: I'm pretty sure Taylor's wife isn't the same Maggie Smith who plays Professor McGonagall in the Harry Potter movies, but maybe?

Zachary Taylor didn't fear things he had not personally experienced. He was a career soldier, so this proved to be valuable; since he'd never experienced death firsthand, he'd never run from it.

Nicknamed Old Rough and Ready by his fellow soldiers due to his alleged roughness and readiness, Taylor achieved fame and praise for his impressive military career. He first landed on America's radar in the War of 1812. In September 1811, Taylor was ordered to escort the eighty men, women, and children under his care (some soldiers, some settlers) from Fort Knox to Fort Harrison, where he would take over command. Unfortunately, the group was struck by malaria, and twenty-four of Taylor's people died. Almost everyone else, including Taylor, was very ill. In an apparent cosmic test of one man's ability to handle one annoying thing after another, just a day or so after Taylor and his people arrived at Fort Harrison, tired and sick and haggard, Taylor got word that hostile Native American forces were planning an attack on the fort.

Of Taylor's remaining men, only about fifteen of them were able soldiers; the rest were either civilian settlers or soldiers who were too ill to fight. Without skipping a beat, Taylor recruited five random settlers and turned them into temporary soldiers. He gave each of the twenty men sixteen rounds of ammunition. On September 4, 1812, Taylor and his men were woken up at midnight when six hundred Native Americans set fire to their camp. The soldiers panicked. (Two of the only healthy soldiers available, in fact, fled the fort as soon as the flames started.) Taylor was disoriented and outnumbered, but by the time the battle started, he was ready to lead. While almost anyone else in the world would have seen two choices (death by fire or death by Native Americans), Taylor, with a handful of troops and a body full of malaria, chose a third option: the Taylor way.

He informed his men that "Taylor never surrenders!" Then Old Rough and Ready calmly ordered some of his men to fix the fort's fire-damaged roof and told the rest to attack the invaders. Taylor saw the flaming fort as a great opportunity, because the flames lit up the sky and revealed the attackers—giving Taylor's men a huge strategic advantage—and because Taylor's crazy. A small chunk of Taylor's men put out the fire and worked to repair the roof while the *other* small chunk of Taylor's men held back the six hundred Native American attackers and provided cover. By morning, the fire was out, the damage was repaired, and the invaders had retreated. It was the first American military victory in the War of 1812, and Taylor pulled it off with a twenty-man, part-civilian army.

Taylor's entire military career is full of similar stories. The Battle of Resaca de la Palma saw a victory under Taylor's command, despite him having only one thousand seven hundred men to Mexico's four thousand. He beat back General Arista's army of twenty thousand with just four thousand five hundred men and what we can only assume is a comical inability to understand how numbers and odds work.

Taylor was a great commander and soldier if you asked his men (despite his high rank, he was always ready and willing to march through swamps or woods or deserts alongside his men and pound on his enemies), but not if you asked his superiors. He had big problems with authority that influenced every decision he made. Even in battle, Taylor refused to dress like a soldier and instead dressed like an angry old rancher, complete with a straw hat and duster coat. Taylor was described as having a permanent scowl, half-closed eyes, wild hair, and coarse features.

Taylor's problem with authority earned him a lot of powerful enemies. When he was given direct orders (either in the War of 1812, or later in the Black Hawk War, or later in the Second Seminole War, or even later in the Holy Moly Zachary Taylor Sure Fought in a Lot of Wars), he often treated them not as commands but as suggestions, which he was always happy to completely ignore.

After forty years of military service, Taylor retired from fighting and reluctantly accepted the Whig nomination for the presidency. And I do mean reluctantly; Taylor once said that the idea of him being president would never "enter the head of any sane person." But we made him president anyway, because he was just so good at killing people. (Our requirements have since broadened.) As president, he was hyperaware that the slavery issue was very quickly going to drive the nation apart. He opposed extending slavery and publicly vowed to personally stomp anyone who disagreed. Literally. Half of the nation vehemently wanted to hold on to their slaves and revolt, and the president of the United States said that he would hang anyone who rebelled against America and do so, according to his biographers, "with less reluctance than he had hanged deserters and spies in Mexico." That's one of the other cool things about Taylor. He never wanted to be president and was pushed into it by the Whigs, who thought, due to his reluctance, that they could control him and use him as a puppet. No one, and I mean *no one* makes a puppet of Taylor. They wanted him to load up his cabinet with big Whigs like Henry Clay, but Taylor ignored these suggestions and instead chose to appoint people with different opinions and backgrounds to reflect the diversity of America herself. Taylor never wanted the job, but that doesn't mean he's just going to sit back and let someone else tell him what to do once he gets it; this is TAYLOR we're talking about.

I know he sounds tough, *unstoppable,* even, but everyone has a weakness, and Taylor's is ridiculous. Taylor died sixteen months into his presidency, but not because he had angered slaveholders in the South, and not because he had angered the Whig Party bosses who nominated him. No, Zachary Taylor was finally defeated by eating too many cherries.

On July 4, 1850, Taylor was at a fund-raising event at the Washington Monument. It was a particularly hot day, and to beat the heat, Taylor decided to eat some cherries. A *lot* of cherries. *Too many* cherries. More cherries than a person is supposed to eat. Historians aren't sure exactly how many cherries he ate, but the very fact that historians are even disputing the exact number of cherries consumed should tell you that it's a pretty freaking serious amount. Taylor got hot and ate an impossible amount of cherries and then washed it down with *way* too much chilled milk.

We will never know why President Zachary Taylor did this. No one has ever prescribed cherries as a solution to overheating, and no one has ever prescribed eating every available cherry in a five-mile radius for *any purpose*. But Taylor was heating up and sincerely believed that the cherries-and-milk combination would

cool him down. Almost immediately after he ate his weight in tiny fruits, Taylor became sick with a mysterious digestive illness and died.

To this day, no one knows exactly what killed Taylor. His doctor diagnosed him with "cholera morbus," which is *barely* a diagnosis. Cholera morbus was a nineteenth-century catchall for a wide spectrum of stomach-related illnesses, including diarrhea, dysentery, and, thanks to Taylor, whatever disease is birthed by the union of digestive fluids and a metric ton of cherries. It was basically his doctor's way of saying, *"His stomach's going nuts and I don't know why."* Some conspiracy theorists maintain that poison was involved, but in 1991, his body was dug up and examined, and all tests for poison came back negative. Anyone with a slightly functioning brain has concluded that it probably had something to do with the lifetime supply of cherries he shoved down his throat on a hot afternoon.

There's no lesson here, apart from "don't eat hundreds of cherries in a single sitting," which is likely something you didn't need someone to teach you to begin with. It's just a superweird thing that happened to a tough guy that we made president. Death by cherries.

OFFICIAL FANTASY DREAM TEAM RATING
He's tough, but, yo . . . cherries. *Cherries.*

13

MILLARD FILLMORE

ONE OF OUR MOST
MILLARD FILLMORE–ESQUE PRESIDENTS

Presidential Term: 1850–1853
Political Party: Whig and Know-Nothing Party
Spouses: Abigail Powers and Caroline Carmichael
Children: Millard Jr. and Mary
Birthdate: January 7, 1800
Death Date: March 8, 1874
Fun Fact: Fillmore has never heard of you either.

There must be some kind of truth to thirteen being unlucky, because Millard Fillmore, our thirteenth president, is as boring as he was terrible. This was bound to happen. Out of all the amazing, brilliant, tough, and exciting presidents we've had, there was bound to be one dud, one president who was lame and crummy in an altogether uninteresting way. Welcome to the Millard Fillmore chapter.

Few men can start with nothing, pick themselves up by their bootstraps, and proclaim proudly, *"Someday, I'm going to be vice president on the off chance that the REAL president dies suddenly and I get to take over the job for him."*

Millard Fillmore was such a man.

It's crazy, because his life story so closely mirrors Abraham Lincoln's (both were born poor in a log cabin, both were mostly self-taught, both were members of the Whig Party early on, both studied law, and both eventually became president), except Fillmore didn't do *any of the cool or noble things that Lincoln did.* He even publicly opposed Lincoln on slavery, because that's high up on the list of things that lame, crummy jerks are supposed to do.

No one wanted Fillmore to be president. Vice presidents are almost never chosen for their popularity or their policies; they're almost *exclusively* chosen to balance out their running mate. The Whigs wanted to run Zachary Taylor, a rough Southern cowboy, for president, which meant they needed a northeastern fancy boy to appeal to the Northern Whigs who would have otherwise been put off by Taylor's brashness. That's it. The Whigs needed someone to balance their candidate who was the opposite of a cowboy war hero, and boy, did they find him.

In case you are reading these chapters out of order, rough and ready President Taylor was felled by a dangerous encounter with a whole mess of cherries. Yes, cherries (see pages 79–81). As soon as Taylor died and Fillmore took office, *the entire cabinet resigned.* Fillmore had a long-standing history of being on the wrong side of important issues (he ran for governor of New York as the "anti-Catholic and anti-immigrant" candidate), and the toxic and divisive issue of slavery was no exception. When Fillmore stepped up to fill in for Taylor, he immediately started supporting the expansion of slavery. The pro-slavery bills Fillmore so staunchly supported became known as the Compromise of 1850. The Compromise, which temporarily eased tensions between the slave-loving South and the abolitionists in the North, caused quite a lot of disagreement in Fillmore's Whig Party. Some, like Lincoln, fled the party for the newly formed Republican Party, and some tried to form their own party while the Whig presence in the South just vanished completely. Whatever Whigs remained agreed on one thing: they did not want to endorse Fillmore as their nominee in the next election. If you feel like the Whigs didn't have a clear objective, you're right. The Whigs were splintering and falling apart, and it simply wasn't a strong-enough party to survive. Like Tyler before him, Fillmore was dropped by his party, but Fillmore's Compromise did more damage than the Whigs could handle. The weakened and scattered Whigs ran one more candidate, Winfield Scott, in the next election, and when he lost in a landslide to Democrat Franklin Pierce, the Whig Party died. No other president can say that he was singularly responsible for destroying a political party (so far).

But here's the *worst* thing Fillmore did. One of those pro-slavery bills Fillmore fought for in the Compromise was the controversial Fugitive Slave Act, which Fillmore signed into law in 1850. Under the Fugitive Slave Act, accused runaway slaves were denied a trial by jury or the right to even testify in court, and essentially any other basic human rights. No documentation was required to prove ownership, by the way. A slaveholder could simply point to a black person and say, *"That guy used to be my slave but he ran away from me,"* and the courts would be satisfied by the owner's word *alone*. As you can imagine, this resulted in the kidnapping and forcing into slavery of many free blacks.

Even if a slave managed to escape his or her owner and make it to a free state, the slave could still be snatched up and returned to the owner, and all citizens were instructed by law to aid in the tracking and retrieval of fugitive slaves. Officers who caught alleged fugitive slaves were offered bonuses and promotions. Judges were encouraged to favor slaveholders. (If a judge ruled in favor of a slave, he would be paid five dollars, but he would be paid *ten* if he ruled in favor of the slaveholder.) Anyone who assisted alleged runaway slaves could face fines or imprisonment because *this was one of the worst laws we've ever had because Fillmore is just awful.*

Fillmore is *also* responsible for the largest treason trial in the history of the United States (again, *so far,* though it's unlikely anyone will top Fillmore). In 1851, a slaveholder (aided by a U.S. marshal) was attempting to capture a fugitive slave in Pennsylvania when a crowd of onlookers formed. The onlookers sided with the slave and refused to help the marshal and slaveholder. Things got hectic and a small fight broke out, and in the chaos, the slave shot and killed his former owner. Fillmore demanded that *all forty-one bystanders* be arrested and charged with treason (though all charges were dismissed by the judge). The Fugitive Slave Act and the Compromise of 1850 temporarily appeased the South, but the Northerners, who were being compelled to enforce slavery against their beliefs, were furious.

Fillmore sought reelection with the Know-Nothing Party, campaigning again as the anti-Catholic/anti-immigrants candidate (he lobbied hard to get Catholics banned from teaching and holding public office), and, needless to say, he lost. It's a good thing too, as Abraham Lincoln maintained that if "the Know-Nothings get control, [the Declaration of Independence] will read 'all men are created equal, except negroes, *and foreigners, and Catholics.'"*

There's not a whole lot more to say about Fillmore. After his presidency, he was offered an honorary Doctor of Civil Law degree by the University of Oxford, but

he declined on the grounds that he had no formal or classical education and, as such, didn't deserve the honor. The diploma was in Latin, and Fillmore maintained that "no man should, in my judgment, accept a degree he cannot read." And, just to make sure he was never on the correct side of history, he spent the remainder of his time in New York publicly criticizing Abraham Lincoln for opposing slavery.

OFFICIAL FANTASY DREAM TEAM RATING

Fillmore's party believed him to be a traitor, as did the citizens of his home state of New York. He's consistently ranked as the fifth or sixth worst president of all time. He signed and obsessively supported the most oppressive law in American history, and his name is really stupid. He has no place on your Fantasy Dream Team.

14

FRANKLIN PIERCE

IS HANDSOME BUT ULTIMATELY USELESS

Presidential Term: 1853–1857

Political Party: Democratic

Spouse: Jane Appleton

Children: Franklin Jr., Frank Robert, and Benjamin

Birthdate: November 23, 1804

Death Date: October 8, 1869

Fun Fact: The practice of "piercing" one's ears does not, in fact, have anything to do with Franklin Pierce. Does this mean there is nothing fun or interesting about Pierce? Probably!

Widely regarded as one of the handsomest presidents, Franklin Pierce was your typical pretty boy, which proves my long-standing theory that pretty boys make terrible presidents. The average American doesn't remember even having a president named Pierce, and most historians, even the ones that go out of their way to be kind to Pierce, admit that there isn't one good achievement that can be credited to his administration.

Not that you should feel *bad* for Pierce. Pierce had a reputation for being incredibly likable his whole life, but behind closed doors, he was a cold jerk—a quality plenty of presidents share but that Pierce owned. His wife, Jane, a lovable and fiercely loyal spouse, only asked him to make one promise to her: to stay out of politics. She saw ambition in her husband's eyes, and as much as she'd support him in almost anything, she hated politics, and with good reason. At this point in American history, it was already clear to many, including Jane, that the presidency was a killer job that took a toll on the president as well as his family. Jane only needed to hear once the stories of Andrew Jackson's wife dying from the grief and stress of being married to a presidential candidate to know that she didn't want any part of it. She didn't want to live in Washington and didn't want her husband consumed by the stress, depression, and long hours that come with a career in politics. Pierce was already a popular player in the Democratic Party (in 1836, he was the youngest U.S. representative at the time), but he left politics and opened up a law office to please his wife.

That was her only request of him. She didn't even lose her cool when he went to go fight in the Mexican-American War without telling her first (even though, *wow*, that's quite a whopper to keep from your wife).

In fairness to Pierce, he *really* wanted to go to war. His greatest frustration was that by the time he had reached his post, the war was almost over. (The "over" part is most soldiers' favorite part of war.) The night before one of the last major battles, Pierce came under enemy fire, was thrown from his horse, and severely injured his knee. His commanding officer honorably discharged him, but Pierce refused to go home and refused to sit out another battle, saying, "This is the last great battle and I *must* lead my brigade!" Say what you want about Pierce, but it takes a special kind of toughness to tell your boss, *"Thanks but no thanks; I think I'd rather spend tomorrow afternoon getting shot at, if it's all the same to you."*

Pierce, weakened but still determined to achieve some battlefield glory, fought in the Battle of Churubusco the next day, almost immediately injuring the same knee. *Of course* he did, because war is very dangerous. His men tried to take him off the field and he *again* refused, because Franklin Pierce invested all his money in blind confidence and was still hoping it would pay sweeping dividends. Even though he couldn't move, Pierce stayed on the battlefield, barking out orders and firing wildly from his place on the ground. He survived this way all through the battle, and his soldiers never forgot it.

And even though Pierce joined the war without telling Jane, and even though he almost got himself killed, she *still* stood by his side, because all she wanted was for him to keep his promise and stay out of politics.

And for many years after the war, he did. He kept his promise and lived a quiet, private life with his loving wife. And then he became president, which, yes, is literally the opposite of not being in politics.

Perhaps claiming that Pierce "lived a quiet, private life" two sentences ago wasn't entirely honest. Even though he wasn't publicly campaigning for office, Pierce stayed in touch with his political buddies in Washington the whole time—quietly, privately making sure they all knew that should someone nominate him, he wouldn't turn down the offer.

It wasn't *just* that he was running a whispered shadow campaign despite his promise to Jane, but that he was doing it all behind her back. Jane was the only person in America in 1852 who didn't know Pierce had his eye on the presidency. The day she found out Pierce was considering stepping into politics was the day a fellow Democrat informed Pierce that he'd received the nomination. The couple was on vacation together, and Jane was absolutely shocked and blindsided by the news. Pierce grinned.

Pierce's decision to sneakily become president against Jane's wishes and behind her back severely damaged their marriage. Tragically, not too long before Pierce was about to move into the White House, the train that carried Franklin, Jane, and their young son went off the rails and crashed. Franklin and Jane survived with just a few scratches, but their son died. This, Jane believed, was punishment for Pierce seeking office when he shouldn't have.

From then on, Jane wore all black every day and stayed away from the White House as often as possible, ignoring her hosting responsibilities. (First Ladies typically hosted lots of parties and entertained guests.) Pierce just kept on presidenting, because that was the kind of man he was. He wanted power and glory, and nothing—not a crushing knee injury or the love of his wife or the loss of his son—was going to get in his way.

Which was weird, because he was a really crappy president. Pierce was more focused on the *job* than he was on the *country*. He spent so much of his time playing the political game and ensuring his spot in the White House that he never looked around to notice that the issue of slavery was very quickly ripping the nation apart, and that the president was going to have to do something about it. We were on the verge of a civil war, and Pierce's inaugural address went on and on about the great period of peace and prosperity taking place in America.

Pierce's not noticing, or at least not understanding, the gravity of the slavery issue was *insane*. As president, he casually repealed the Missouri Compromise, which prohibited slavery in Kansas. With this statute out of the way, the Kansas and Nebraska Territories were now allowed to decide for themselves whether they'd join the Union as free states or slave states, which set in motion a series of violent battles in the territory known as Bleeding Kansas.

He was also arrested while president for running over a woman with his horse, but he was discharged due to a lack of sufficient evidence. This doesn't relate to any grand, meaningful truth about Pierce and it doesn't tie into anything about his character, his administration, or anything; it's just crazy. A president got arrested. For a horse accident. That's nuts. Anyway . . .

Like Millard Fillmore before him, Pierce was not nominated by his party after his first term. The anti-slavery members of the Democratic Party turned on Pierce when he vocally supported slavery as president, a fact he'd hidden from them during the nomination process. Pierce has mostly been forgotten by the average

American, but it's important to note that his support for the repeal of the Missouri Compromise is one of the most damaging decisions a president has ever made.

Pierce also had a drinking problem that plagued him his entire life, and it only worsened when he became president. Jane's love and support had kept him away from the bottle, but with her frequent absence from the White House, there was nothing to stop him from abusing alcohol whenever he felt stressed, depressed, or really *any* other emotion. The tragedy of losing his son coupled with the added anxieties of leading a divided nation made his drinking worse. When he left the White House and someone asked him what his postpresidency plans were, Pierce replied, "The only thing left to do is get drunk," and that's exactly what he did, until it destroyed his liver enough to kill him.

OFFICIAL FANTASY DREAM TEAM RATING

It is not advisable to add Pierce to your Fantasy Dream Team. If you based your decision solely on his sneaky early political plotting, he would seem like a good candidate for the **Brains,** but his weak presidency and his crumbling in the face of a looming civil war shows that he just can't handle the pressure.

15

JAMES BUCHANAN

MAN OF MYSTERY

Presidential Term: 1857–1861

Political Party: Democratic

Spouse: None

Children: None

Birthdate: April 23, 1791

Death Date: June 1, 1868

Fun Fact: Buchanan had an almost superhuman ability to hear and confessed that he could hear conversations going on *through walls*.

James Buchanan has the build of a fighter but the spirit of a bed wetter. It was under his watch that America first split into two. The law of odds guarantees that *someone* had to be president when America's North and South faced off on the issue of slavery, so it's not Buchanan's *fault* that it happened in the first place, but he's still one of the worst people to be president when it *did* happen. Modern historians have voted his failure in the face of secession as the worst presidential mistake ever made. His do-nothing attitude and his inability to take a firm stance on slavery left the South no other choice, and history would have been wildly different if Buchanan hadn't been running our country at the birth of the Civil War.

Buchanan's worthless presidency is a real shame, not just because it damaged the country, but because Buchanan showed such early promise as a cool tough guy. In college he could often be found breaking university policy by smoking cigars and drinking to excess on campus in the middle of the day, getting into trouble (he was temporarily expelled), and ticking off his teachers, because even though he clearly wasn't studying or taking school seriously, he was still getting better grades than *almost everyone*. He did well enough in school that he earned a special academic honor, but because he was a jerk about it, his professors got together and decided not to give it to him on graduation day. He'd be worth celebrating for his coolness, if only he hadn't eventually indirectly caused the Civil War.

Buchanan cleaned up his rebellious streak after college and enjoyed a series of very successful careers before his presidency. He lived by his often-repeated personal slogan, "I acknowledge no master but the law," whose similarity to "I am the law" makes James Buchanan our most Judge Dreddian president to date.

Buchanan rode his "cool college kid" reputation all the way to the White House. He threw a TON of parties as president and even wrote to the official presidential liquor supplier once to complain that the bottles of champagne and whiskey they were sending weren't large enough. ("Pints," Buchanan wrote, "are very inconvenient in this house, as the article is not used in such small quantities.")

Buchanan may have been a world-class partier, but he didn't leave the country with much to celebrate. It's easy to say that the Civil War was inevitable, and the war didn't officially start until Lincoln's presidency, but *secession* started under Buchanan. When people talked of secession to Andrew Jackson, he threatened to hang every last one of them. This is where Buchanan's "no master but the law" mantra hurts him, because when people talked of secession on Buchanan's watch, he felt that the law did not allow him to stop them. Buchanan believed that while it was unconstitutional for states to secede, it was *also* unconstitutional for him as president to stop them. It was a cop-out. Buchanan was basically saying, *"Don't secede because it's against the law, even though I won't do anything if you break it, because doing something is also against the law. So . . . please?"* South Carolina chose to secede almost immediately, because *of course they did*. They asked Buchanan to remove Northern troops from South Carolina's Fort Sumter, and he would have had one of his cabinet members not pointed out that giving in to the South at this point in history would be *an act of treason.*

With America falling apart around him, Buchanan got frustrated and turned to his cabinet, fussing and nosily interfering with the personal lives of his staffers and their wives. The South was threatening secession and seizing forts, and Buchanan just wanted to gossip and drink and throw parties and dance until his term was up. He couldn't *wait* to leave the White House.

Unspectacular as a president, Buchanan remains very interesting and mysterious as a man. While he never married, he did have one early romance and even got engaged to a woman named Ann Coleman. Their engagement ended suddenly, and then his would-be fiancée left town and died mysteriously. Her doctor recorded her cause of death as hysteria, but since there had never been a previous case of "death by hysteria" reported, he admitted in his report that he suspected her death to be a possible suicide, caused by a self-inflicted overdose of opiates. No one knows why Buchanan and Ann broke up, and no one knows why or if she killed herself or what role he played, if any, but the situation was suspicious enough that Ann's father forbade Buchanan from attending her funeral.

As if things weren't weird already, Buchanan made everything much crazier.

To close friends and members of the Coleman family, Buchanan promised that one day everything would be explained. In a letter to Ann's father after her death, he cryptically wrote, "It is now no time for explanation, but the time will come when you discover that she, as well as I, have been much abused." Buchanan similarly stated that he wrote a letter that would explain the strange circumstances surrounding his broken engagement, Ann's death, and his subsequent ban from attending Ann's funeral, but that the letter containing these answers was sealed in an envelope that could not be opened until his death. Shortly before he died from respiratory failure in 1868, he changed his mind and instructed his niece to burn this and every other letter she could find. We'll never know what the letter said, why Buchanan's former fiancée may have killed herself, or what his big revelation would have been. The only informed conclusion to draw from this whole story is that Buchanan was weird, paranoid, and *mysterious as heck*. History remembers Buchanan as one of our worst presidents (and his critics at the time often called the Civil War Buchanan's War), but history should *also* remember Buchanan as a man who left bizarre chains of secret letters and could hear through walls. Because that's objectively way cooler.

Buchanan could have been a great president, but at the end of the day, he choked. He had a greater intellectual capacity than almost any president before or after him, and he was charming and perceptive, but when the going got tough, he faltered.

OFFICIAL FANTASY DREAM TEAM RATING

There's no room for Buchanan on your roster.

16

ABRAHAM LINCOLN

OUR MUTANT PRESIDENT

Presidential Term: 1861–1865

Political Party: Republican

Spouse: Mary Todd

Children: Robert, Edward, William, and Thomas

Birthdate: February 12, 1809

Death Date: April 15, 1865

Fun Fact: Lincoln LOVED telling filthy, hilarious jokes.

Abraham Lincoln, the sixteenth president of the United States, was superhuman.

I'm not just saying he was tall (though, at six feet four inches, he is still our tallest and fourth-beardiest president). I'm saying that physically, he possibly had a disease called Marfan syndrome, or a related genetic disorder called MEN2B. (I say "possibly" because no one was around to diagnose the disease at the time.) People who suffer from Marfan syndrome generally grow taller than the average person and have longer limbs that are typically fairly weak. Lincoln refused to accept the "weak" part of his condition and strengthened his arms through years of farmwork (he built his first log cabin when he was *freaking seven*), because why even *have* bonus arms if you're not going to make them the strongest and most powerful arms you can? A life full of log splitting made Lincoln so strong that by the time he was twenty-two, his skills were already *legendary*. His cousin Dennis Hanks, who lived in Lincoln's town of New Salem, Illinois, said, "if you heard his fellin' trees in a clearin' you would say there was three men at work by the way the trees fell." But it wasn't three men. It was just one giant superpresident. Lincoln's neighbors would see him down by the riverbank using his extra-strength arms to lift a box of stones that weighed "one thousand pounds," according to some townsfolk.

I'm not saying that there's an age when someone *should* be strong enough to regularly carry around one-thousand-pound boulders (that's far too much power for one man), but twenty-two still feels aggressively, dangerously young for that amount of strength. If you ever see a twenty-two-year-old carrying a boulder that weighs anything close to one thousand pounds, you'd better make him president.

Having supertough arms wasn't Lincoln's only superpower; I'm saying that Lincoln might have been able to see the future. The year of his presidential election, Lincoln dreamed he saw two reflections of his face in the mirror. One looked normal and the other was pale, gaunt, and awful-looking. He consulted with his wife, Mary Todd, and they concluded that this meant he would survive his first but not his second term. And if that wasn't ominous enough, one week before his assassination, he had a dream that involved waking up in the White House to the sound of crying. He traced the source of the crying to the East Wing, where a number of soldiers stood around a corpse covered with a sheet. He asked, "Who is dead in the White House?" and a soldier responded, "The [p]resident, he was killed by an assassin." If Mr. Fantastic and Jean Grey had a baby (which would cause *tons* of questions), it would be Abraham Lincoln.

But before all that, before all the stuff that you know about Lincoln, you should know that he was a *fighter*. When he moved to New Salem in his early twenties, Lincoln quickly made a name for himself by finding the toughest guy in town, Jack Armstrong, and immediately challenging him to a fight. Armstrong had Lincoln beat in terms of fighting experience and name coolness, but Lincoln, of course, had him beat in two very important categories: (a) mutant powers and (b) being Abraham Lincoln.

Using his massive arms (the ones that carried one-thousand-pound boulders all over town), Lincoln grabbed Armstrong by the throat, lifted him off his feet, shook him like a child, and then tossed him when he surrendered. *Tossed him.*

Armstrong's friends jumped in to gang up on Lincoln, who just laughed and laughed. Well, he didn't *just* laugh. He laughed for a little bit, and then he beat up all of them. *All of them.* You see, Jack Armstrong and his friends actually *were* a gang called the Clary's Grove Boys, and they terrorized the town of New Salem with intimidation and drunken aggression. No one seemed to be able to stand up to them, so they basically ran the whole place. Lincoln came in, saw this unruly gang of thugs terrorizing the town, and inside of a week, mopped the floor with every single one of them. He saw what they were doing and probably said something like, *"Hey, I know I'm brand-new in town, but I'm going to keep shaking your toughest guys until you all respect me"*—and then he threw Jack Armstrong into space in lieu of verbal explanation.

By the way, Lincoln made good use of all that early fighting and crowd control. Years after his fight with Armstrong, in his very first campaign speech for public office in New Salem, Lincoln spotted a verbal fight break out in the crowd between a Lincoln supporter and a Lincoln critic. Instead of politely asking the unruly audience member to quiet down (like literally *any* other politician hoping to convince voters he's trustworthy and coolheaded), Lincoln left the stage, walked into the audience, picked the man up, and threw him twelve feet.

Lincoln wasn't just a jerk-hurling president with monster arms (though that would be a perfectly adequate legacy if that were the case); he was also a ticking time bomb of ambition. Everyone loves to talk about how Lincoln was born poor in a log cabin, but he *hated* that part of his life and wanted nothing more than to rise above it as quickly as possible. He wanted to be remembered and he wanted the respect of his fellow man, but mostly he wanted *power*. He was obsessed with power and ambition—that's why Lincoln took his first position in public office (a seat in the state legislature) when he was just twenty-five years old, despite not having a job, a house, any money, or more than one year of formal education. He ran for office with absolutely no prospects, believing, perhaps, that he would just eat power to stay alive.

Four days into Lincoln's first session in the legislature, he introduced his first bill. The next day he started writing bills for *other* legislators. Lincoln was a man who wrote laws despite never having taken a law class in his entire life. He also never lost his fury. While still a public servant, he would verbally attack Democratic opponents, and when a critic spoke out about Lincoln's bills, he threatened "to give his proboscis a good wringing," which is the classiest way on record to say, "I'm going to punch you in the nose."

Lincoln hated slavery on a deeply personal level, and he was frustrated that, unlike most things he hated, slavery wasn't the kind of thing he could simply lift up by the throat and shake until it was no longer a threat. Instead, he had to content himself with attacking slavery the legal and political way. He also saw slavery as an opportunity—an issue he could use to make his name. He knew he wasn't going to be a war hero and he knew he wasn't rich, so the only way for him to stand out was to take a bold, public stance on a divisive issue, and slavery was just the ticket. He passionately spoke out against slavery and rode the fame it gave him to the position of chairman of the state legislature, and when that wasn't enough, president of the United States. And, when *that* wasn't enough, he decided to become one of the *greatest* presidents of the United States. Currently Lincoln spends all his time alternately haunting our money and appreciating the many monuments we've made in his honor from whatever position of power he no doubt holds in heaven (vice God?).

But before all that, Lincoln exercised more power as president than any man before or since. Four months into his first term, he increased the size of the army by twenty-two thousand and the size of the navy by eighteen thousand, and he demanded a draft calling for forty thousand more men (the first draft in American history). He suspended the writ of habeas corpus (a legal action that stops people in power, like presidents, from arresting whomever they want) and proceeded to arrest whomever he wanted (in Lincoln's case, that meant over ten thousand Southern sympathizers). He made the arrests public both to help the war effort *and* to send a message to everyone that he wasn't to be messed with. He delayed Congress for four months so no one could stop him, and when it was time for reelection, he made all federal employees give 3 percent of their paycheck to his campaign.

Presidents, especially modern presidents, have so many eyes on them and so many people to answer to, and a Congress that is often stubborn and difficult to deal with. There are so many checks and balances in place that today it would be laughable to accuse a president of being a tyrant. While I'm not calling *Lincoln* a tyrant, I *am* saying that he did whatever he wanted for over four years. You know, like a tyrant.

Since Lincoln clearly wasn't going to let Congress or public opinion stop him or even inform his policies, perhaps you're thinking that his wife could have had

some influence. Unfortunately, Mary Todd Lincoln's life was very tragic. She and Lincoln had already lost their son Eddie to pneumonia before Lincoln became president. Then, while they were living in the White House, their son Willie died from typhoid fever when he was just eleven years old, and Mary Todd never totally recovered from it. She suffered from depression and often met with psychics in an attempt to communicate with her departed sons. Lincoln even accompanied her

on a few of these visits, mostly to confirm that these "psychics" were, in fact, con artists taking advantage of a grieving woman. She also had migraines and was prone to mood swings and emotional outbursts, prompting Lincoln to threaten at least once to have her institutionalized (though he never followed through). As if watching two sons die wasn't enough, Mary Todd was with her husband when *he* died at the hands of John Wilkes Booth. Unbelievably, she then had to suffer through the death of a third son, Thomas—whom they called Tad—from tuberculosis at age eighteen. All these tragedies were too much for Mary Todd. In later years she grew paranoid and delusional, and she was temporarily institutionalized by her sole remaining son, Robert. Upon leaving the hospital, she unsuccessfully attempted suicide before dying in 1882 at sixty-three years old.

There's ample evidence to suggest that Lincoln *also* suffered from depression, which just makes his performance as president even more impressive. He suffered great losses and was dealing with a grieving and unhappy wife, and he *still* managed to fight a war and keep the country together during the worst period of America's history.

OFFICIAL FANTASY DREAM TEAM RATING

Stick Lincoln in *any* position and you really can't go wrong. He's got a strong-enough mind that he saw the way to American peace *and* emancipation when no one else could (**Brains**). He wasn't afraid to pull out all the stops when he thought it necessary (**Loose Cannon**), always fought for what he believed in (**Moral Compass**), and could *literally throw his opponents away* (**Brawn**). Lincoln should absolutely be your first or second draft pick.

17
ANDREW JOHNSON
PRESIDENT UNDERDOG

Presidential Term: 1865–1869
Political Party: Democratic
Spouse: Eliza McCardle
Children: Martha, Charles, Mary, Robert, and Andrew Jr.
Birthdate: December 29, 1808
Death Date: July 31, 1875
Fun Fact: Johnson was buried with his body wrapped in the
American flag and a worn copy of the Constitution as his pillow.
We get it, Andrew, *you love America.*

Andrew Johnson, our seventeenth president, just could not catch a break. Ever. If there was ever a president who could be called our Charlie Browniest, it would be Andrew Johnson. Sure, he was president, so clearly there are worse fates to have, but from the minute he was born until the minute he died, Andrew Johnson was an underdog who never belonged *anywhere*. Born poor and raised without a father, Johnson never attended school and was sold as an indentured servant to a tailor when he was just a boy. His poverty made him an outsider in his own town of Raleigh, North Carolina, and he had to put up with being called poor white trash throughout his entire childhood. He taught himself to read and write, worked hard, and was kind to the people he met. But he never really overcame his low background, not in Raleigh, anyway. Still, he wouldn't let his detractors get to him; he was just going to keep his head down, stay sharp, and work hard. "Honest conviction is my courage," Johnson used to say.

While he was an indentured servant, Johnson studied, read, and learned all about being a tailor, until, seeing bigger plans for himself, he ran away at the age of fifteen. His "employer" placed an ad in a newspaper, offering a ten-dollar reward to anyone who returned him, but Johnson was not captured. Johnson struck out on his own as a tailor in Carthage, North Carolina. He eventually made enough money to go back and pay off his apprenticeship, and he continued to work as a tailor for several years before starting a career in politics. He served as a mayor, a senator, and eventually the governor of Tennessee, but unfortunately for him, he didn't fit in there either. As a Southerner who supported the Union during the Civil War, Johnson was hated by all of Tennessee, even though his position was basically *"Hey, I like having slaves too, but wouldn't it be better if we weren't all killing each other?"* It might seem strange that someone so disliked would even get elected as governor, but because this is Johnson we're talking about, you have to assume that even his governorship is fairly Charlie Browny. A Tennessee governor in the 1800s was mostly powerless, *especially* a Charlie Brown one like Johnson. The Whig Party, while clearly on its way out around the country, was still very much alive in Tennessee. Johnson couldn't veto anything because the Tennessee legislature was still mostly controlled by Whigs, and he didn't even really have the power to make any political appointments or influence legislation. He used his position as governor to raise his own profile so he could hopefully one day occupy the higher offices he actually sought, while everyone around him refused to call him the governor without rolling their eyes or throwing up sarcastic air quotes when they said it.

Johnson moved on to the U.S. Senate, but despite his best efforts, Tennessee seceded in 1861. Most Southern sympathizers with the Union fled when their state seceded, but Johnson stayed in town to serve as military governor, a position appointed to him by President Lincoln—a man whose authority a Confederate state like Tennessee didn't even recognize. This meant that he had the very difficult job of having to hold the state together and punish anyone who was anti-Union, which involved shutting down Confederate newspapers, firing anyone in his office that didn't support the president, and arresting pro-secession members of the clergy. Needless to say, this didn't exactly make him a hometown hero. He stayed in Nashville, which was constantly under attack by Confederate rebels trying to seize control, but he never let them take over, at one point swearing to his panicked staff that "any one who talks of surrender I will shoot." By the end of the war, Johnson had restored civil government in Tennessee, but that didn't stop the people from hanging ANDREW JOHNSON: TRAITOR banners all over town. Believing that "despised military governor" was at least sort of a step up from "powerless pretend governor," Johnson again kept his head down, worked hard, and continued to do what he thought was right.

You might be wondering why such an unspectacular and almost universally disrespected man like Andrew Johnson was even chosen as vice president to begin with. Johnson was chosen by Lincoln because Johnson was a Southerner, and Lincoln wanted to send the message that he would be willing to work with the South should the Civil War not go his way. It was, again, a decision based solely on balancing the ticket, but historians still rate the Johnson appointment as the worst move of Lincoln's political career.

If you ask the average person what he or she thinks of when thinking about Johnson, the answer will either be his impeachment or his drunkenness. Johnson was a good man and a hard worker, but he developed a reputation for being a drunk. Why? Probably because he was totally drunk when he delivered his inauguration speech as vice president. That's probably the reason.

Johnson's speech, described by the *New York Herald* as "remarkable for its incoherence," was all about the important lessons he learned growing up poor, how great the country is, and other thoughts common to very drunk people. Various staffers tried to shush or pull him off the stage, but he wasn't having it, speaking ten minutes longer than he was scheduled to. A senator at the time, Zachariah Chandler, said, "The Vice President Elect was too drunk to perform his duties and disgraced himself and the Senate by making a drunken foolish speech. I was never so mortified in my life, had I been able to find a hole I would have dropped through it out of sight." Johnson wanted to make America feel beautiful that day, so he ended his speech by saying, "I kiss this Book in the face of my nation of the United States," then *drunkenly kissed the Bible on which he took his oath.*

Of course, that's only half the story. Even though Johnson was completely drunk for his wild, rambling speech, it wasn't because he was an alcoholic by any means. Most people who knew Johnson knew him to have a drink or two once in a while, but that's about it. In this particular case, Johnson had been sick for several months with typhoid fever, and his doctor had prescribed him a few shots of whiskey. (Medicine in the 1800s, man. What a fun time.) Obviously the combination of the whiskey and his illness produced that absurd speech. The story could have ended there, but history is written by the winners (also by me!), and all the winners *hated* Andrew Johnson. His critics were loud and persistent, and that's how Andrew Johnson, a self-made man who picked himself up and worked hard his whole life, went down in history as the drunken vice president.

Even the fact that Johnson became president at the time he did is completely unfair in some grand, cosmic sort of way. Being president is never easy, but Johnson had to step up and fill in for one of the greatest presidents we've ever had during Reconstruction, one of the roughest periods in our history. If Johnson had followed, say, Fillmore or Pierce or one of those other "lesser presidents," history would likely remember him more fondly. Unfortunately, his opening act was Lincoln, and that's a performance *no one* can follow. It would be like following the Beatles, except the audience hates you, and instead of being as good as or better than the Beatles, your band is *Andrew Johnson*.

As a president, Johnson was as disrespected as he was as a governor, military governor, and human being, which is to say, *very*. His secretary of war, Edwin Stanton, vocally opposed Johnson's Reconstruction efforts and actively undermined his president's decisions in the South. (Johnson wanted civil authorities to have control over the South, but Stanton wanted military leaders in control.) Johnson, who was trying to heal a wounded nation *and* live up to Lincoln's legacy, had enough to deal with already and didn't need some uppity secretary of war second-guessing him at every turn, so he asked for Stanton's resignation. Stanton refused. Then Congress, who *also* didn't respect Johnson, passed the Reconstruction Act, which (a) took away Johnson's control over the U.S. Army in the South and (b) took away Johnson's ability to fire any cabinet members without the approval of the Senate. It was a move specifically designed to protect Stanton's position, and when Johnson tried to fire Stanton anyway—ignoring the Reconstruction Act because it seemed unconstitutional to him, and also because *"Come on, just give me a break, guys"*—he was impeached. He managed to keep his job by *one single vote,* but the writing on the wall was clear. The people never wanted or expected Johnson to be president, his Congress hated him, and even his own cabinet members ignored and disobeyed him. Johnson was, again, on his own.

It probably goes without saying that the Johnson presidency was unspectacular, but hey, let's say it anyway. Johnson's presidency was unspectacular. Johnson purchased Alaska for America, which was great, but this sort of paled in comparison to Lincoln's slave-freeing, war-ending one-two punch. It's also worth pointing out that Johnson wasn't just some unlucky, lovable underdog; he was also on the wrong side of history (which is very difficult to do when you're Abraham Lincoln's vice president). As president, Johnson vocally fought against the Fourteenth

Amendment, the one that recognized blacks as citizens. Even though Johnson had freed his own slaves and supported the Union during the Civil War, he had a deep and intense dislike of blacks. When Frederick Douglass, the famous black abolitionist, first met Johnson, he described the look on Johnson's face as "one of bitter contempt and aversion" and Johnson himself as "no friend of our race." And Johnson's "Reconstruction efforts" that Congress opposed, which we discussed earlier? They were all designed to keep the South as a white-dominated land where blacks could legally be considered second-class citizens. If Johnson *had* been impeached, that might have actually been *huge* for America, but we'll never know.

OFFICIAL FANTASY DREAM TEAM RATING

Nope! Nope! Noooooope! You don't want Johnson on your side.

THE PRESIDENTIAL ★ SCORECARD

? Brains
? Brawn
? Loose Cannon
? Moral Compass
? Roosevelt...

18

ULYSSES S. GRANT

IS THE DRUNKEN, ANGRY JOHN McCLANE OF PRESIDENTS

Presidential Term: 1869–1877
Political Party: Republican
Spouse: Julia Dent
Children: Frederick, Ulysses Jr., Ellen, and Jesse
Birthdate: April 27, 1822
Death Date: July 23, 1885
Fun Fact: Grant's real first name was Hiram, and Ulysses was his middle name. The "S" actually stood for absolutely nothing.

Ulysses S. Grant was put on this earth to do two things: win battles and drink booze. And that's not an exaggeration; Grant was a failure at almost everything else he tried to do. He was never a great student, he was never an athlete, and he didn't have many friends. He wasn't a terrific communicator, and as president, he didn't make enough of an impact to turn heads on any historical polls.

Grant wasn't even a solid military strategist, which is probably why he won so much. What Grant had, and what almost any great general needs, was a deep, natural, and impossible-to-quantify instinct for war. It is an unteachable skill that combines instinct with practicality and total ruthlessness, and Grant had it in spades. He never so much as picked up a book on strategy and never based any decisions he made on the battlefield on an attempt to be one step ahead of the other guy; he just operated with a sort of primitive war IQ. Grant was simply surviving by fighting every single day and every single night; he was a mad fighter full of piss and vinegar, and lots of whiskey.

Oh, right, the drinking. Nothing could stop Grant from drinking—not an important battle, and not even the soldier Grant personally hired to stop him from drinking too much. Let's say that again. Grant knew that he drank so much that he appointed *an armed soldier* specifically to make sure he didn't drink during the war, and still he drank—and he *might have been right for doing so*. The drinking lowered Grant's inhibitions and helped him keep his cool in any situation. Even President Lincoln admitted that he wanted Grant in command of the army specifically *because* of his drinking. He was an alcoholic, but he was, according to Lincoln, exactly the kind of alcoholic the Union needed.

His constant drunkenness combined with his terrifying innate battle prowess made him impossibly great as a soldier and later as commander of the Union army, and by "impossibly great," I do mean that he objectively should not have been as successful as he was. He was regularly going up against generals who had more experience and skill and sobriety, and like Washington before him, he would often return from battle unscathed despite having his horse shot out from under him, or his sword shot right out of his hand. He won because he was lucky, full of liquid courage, and stubborn. Grant admitted on more than one occasion to having an inability to turn back in battle after choosing to advance, an aversion based entirely on his own superstitions. He thought it was bad luck to retreat, so he fought and he fought and he fought and he *fought*.

There are also some . . . weirder facts about Hiram. Grant drank as much as he did because he was cripplingly insecure, especially about being naked. All his fellow soldiers would shower outside together in the morning, and Grant was the only one who refused to be seen naked by any of his men. He would bathe himself alone in his tent, and not a single other soldier (not even his aides or helpers) was allowed to see him (quite unlike John Quincy Adams, who swam naked every day).

It wasn't just being naked that made Grant uncomfortable. For someone who made a career out of killing people and helping other people kill people, he was notoriously squeamish when it came to blood. He hated the sight and taste of it so much that on the rare occasions when he did eat meat, he demanded that it be burned to a near crisp.

As president, Grant had a pretty difficult time. He was a career soldier who never really dreamed of being president, and he happened to get the job during

Reconstruction, one of America's darkest periods. While Grant himself wasn't a dishonest man, his *office* was plagued with corruption. Still, Grant should be remembered as perhaps one of the first civil rights presidents. While Johnson urged Southerners to deny political and civil rights to blacks, Grant conversely pushed for the ratification of the Fourteenth Amendment and the Fifteenth Amendment, which granted blacks the right to vote. It was during Grant's administration that over three thousand members of the Ku Klux Klan were indicted and the military was sent to the South to stop racist whites from lynching, beating, and kidnapping blacks. Grant said, "Treat the negro as a citizen and a voter, as he is and must remain, and soon parties will be divided, not on the color line, but on principle."

He was also, unlike the many grizzled war heroes-turned-presidents before him, refreshingly tolerant of Native Americans, whom he called the original inhabitants of this land, and wrote to his wife to say that "the whole race would be

harmless and peaceable if they were not put upon by whites." Perhaps growing up being rejected by his parents and disliked by others in his age group (his nickname was Useless) filled Grant with empathy for the underdog. He encouraged the Native Americans to get American citizenship, respected all treaties (even though most previous administrations ignored them), and got Congress to provide financial aid to fund Native American education.

He also loved animals! What a sweet guy. Grant rode and loved horses, and he spent all his time outside bonding with and talking to animals, the only creatures that couldn't reject him. He loved animals *so* much that when he caught a teamster whipping a horse in the face during the Battle of the Wilderness (part of the Civil War in 1864), he flew into a rage, used profanity (for the only time in his life), tied the man to a tree, and left him there for six hours. It was the angriest anyone had ever seen Grant, and he was one of our deadliest generals. If you so much as step on a spider while in Grant's presence, you'll unleash an inner Hulk that you don't want to mess with.

OFFICIAL FANTASY DREAM TEAM RATING

With his drunkenness, stubbornness, and unwillingness to lose, Grant would be a great pick for your **Loose Cannon,** a man on whom you can rely to make the tough decisions to get the job *done*. Just don't ask him to do it naked.

19

RUTHERFORD B. HAYES

IS BAD AT LOSING

Presidential Term: 1877–1881
Political Party: Republican
Spouse: Lucy Webb
Children: Birchard, Webb, Rutherford, Joseph, George, Fanny,
Scott, and Manning (Those are some WEIRD names.
"Birchard"? Get outta town.)
Birthdate: October 4, 1822
Death Date: January 17, 1893
Fun Fact: Hayes was the first president who actually *lost* the popular vote!

Rutherford B. Hayes is one of the lesser-known presidents, but he's also the most likely to kick your butt as soon as you count him out. He's one of the last in a long run of truly tough presidents, old-school men who chomped cigars and fought in wars. Hayes served in over fifty skirmishes in the Civil War and was shot several times, but nothing seemed to slow him down.

In 1862, as lieutenant colonel in one battle, Hayes was severely injured. He was shot in the left arm; the bullet splintered one of his forearm bones and tore a blood vessel. Hayes lost a ton of blood, but instead of bleeding to death like a normal person, "he continued to give direction to his troops and succeeded in scattering the rebels." He collapsed to the ground and, between rounds of vomiting, called out orders and even yelled at his men if they seemed to be behaving cowardly. He did all of this from a very exposed position while bleeding on the ground.

In another battle, Hayes had his horse shot out from under him and was thrown several feet while a bullet grazed his skull, and most of his men assumed he was dead. Instead he was just knocked out, and as soon as he regained consciousness, he shook off the fall (and bullet wound to the head), found a new horse, and just started fighting again.

That battle was in 1864, by the way, two years *after* Hayes got his arm shot up and doctors almost had to amputate it. Most soldiers would have just left the army honorably after an injury like Hayes's, but he recovered and got right back to the fight. That might seem like an impossibly short amount of time, but it was par for the course for Hayes. From birth Hayes was a weak and sickly child, so sick that his mother was afraid to show him any love; she assumed she'd lose him, and she didn't want to get attached. As a result, Hayes (whose father died before he was born) drove himself to excellence to win her love. He wouldn't be held back by his sickness or his father being dead and his mother ignoring him; he was going to grow up to be big and strong and *president*. He started a daily fitness regimen as a child that lasted until the week he died; even as president, he would wake up with the roosters and start exercising. Historians said that as a child, he developed "an unusual strength and muscular coordination," and it was this unusual strength that helped him in battle and allowed him to survive despite being shot *five times* in the Civil War.

Hayes wasn't just supposed to lose his young life and his later battles; he was also supposed to lose the presidential election. 1876 saw the end of the Grant administration, and while Grant himself was an honest and decent man, his administration was one of the most corrupt in American history. This was a time when reform was important, so the Democrats nominated Samuel Tilden, a successful reformer who fought corruption as the governor of New York. The Republicans picked Rutherford B. Hayes, who wasn't so much a "successful reformer" as he was just "some guy."

Hayes was chosen not for his policies, or his ability to speak, or his track record, but because he hadn't yet stolen anything or annoyed anyone. Hayes's history of being a strong soldier was just a bonus; really the "not doing anything wrong" thing was what made him attractive to his party. The Republicans just wanted someone who had never stolen (which prompted journalist Joseph Pulitzer to yell, "Good God! Has it come to this?"). Hayes had a clean record and was generally inoffensive. Generally inoffensive? What more can we ask for? Let's make him president.

When Election Day rolled around and the votes started coming in, it was clear to just about everybody that Tilden had won—Hayes had lost the popular vote by over 300,000 votes and even wrote a concession speech. America would never hear it. Once the Republicans realized there were four states left to count (and that Hayes could win the Electoral College [the Electoral College is the system that— You know what? Ask your parents.] if he carried those states), they sent people armed with hundreds of thousands of dollars (and weapons) to make sure everyone voted correctly (in this case, "correctly" means "Republican"). Republicans called vote counters in South Carolina, offering anywhere between $30,000 and $200,000 for a Republican victory. An entire box of votes favoring Tilden in Key West, Florida, was *straight up thrown out*.

The threats and bribery and back-alley dealing went on for weeks, until a special committee was chosen to decide the election. The committee had eight Republicans and seven Democrats, so the Republicans won and Rutherford "At Least I Never Stole Anything" Hayes stole the presidency. (This earned him the nickname Rutherfraud, which, admittedly, is a more succinct nickname.) Hayes ended up being a decent president, seeing America through the end of Reconstruction, but he didn't make any friends in office and didn't do anything as president that was either scandalous enough to give him villain status or exciting and progressive enough to give him hero status in the history books. Tired of the life of a politician, he chose not to seek reelection.

It's fitting that Hayes's death was more rad than the *lives* of most people. He was still strong and physically active in retirement, but life caught up with him. On January 14, 1893, seventy-one-year-old Hayes suffered a minor heart issue while riding a train to Cleveland. According to his travel companion, Hayes briefly complained of the pain, then shook it off and casually sipped brandy. The "minor heart issue"? It was a heart attack—he just hadn't realized it. No one did, in fact; doctors didn't even find out until they examined his body and medical history years later.

He had a heart attack, prescribed himself brandy, went home, and died *three days later,* on January 17.

OFFICIAL FANTASY DREAM TEAM RATING

Hayes, who was known to say that "fighting battles is like courting girls: those who make the most pretensions and are boldest usually win," would be a pretty strong candidate for your **Brawn** position. He just didn't know how to lose, regardless of the odds. He *should* have died as a sick, fatherless child. He *should* have died from his wounds in the Civil War. He *should* have lost the election, because he literally *did* lose the election. Yet Hayes still came out on top. You'd be wise to keep a guy like that around.

THE PRESIDENTIAL ★ SCORECARD

- ? Brains
- ? Brawn
- ? Loose Cannon
- ? Moral Compass
- ? Roosevelt...

20

JAMES GARFIELD

THE PRESIDENT WHO WAS BARELY THERE

Presidential Term: 1881
Political Party: Republican
Spouse: Lucretia Rudolph
Children: Eliza, Harry, James, Mary, Irvin, Abram, and Edward
Birthdate: November 19, 1831
Death Date: September 19, 1881
Fun Fact: Garfield was ambidextrous!

James Garfield's presidency was cut so short (he was assassinated just four months into his term) that most historians don't even include him when they're ranking the best and worst presidents; there's simply not enough information to figure out his legacy. Luckily for us, there's plenty of information about Garfield's career as an awesome dude.

Garfield grew up poor and without a father (his father died when he was just eighteen months old) in Ohio, and was the last president born in a log cabin (unless they somehow become cool again). His schoolmates relentlessly mocked him for his fatherless status, because children are literally the worst people in the world. (Garfield claimed he was "made the ridicule and sport of boys that had fathers, and enjoyed the luxuries of life.") The only thing Garfield knew about his father, Abram, was that he was an accomplished wrestler, so Garfield learned early on how to defend himself, earning the nickname the Fighting Kid.

Garfield never grew out of fighting either. Years later, when Garfield ran into a guy who "refused to obey" him, Garfield reportedly "flogged him severely," and the guy attacked Garfield with a plank of wood for what Garfield described as "a merry time." Garfield retaliated with glee, after which the guy "vamoosed." I keep calling his attacker a "guy," but that should probably be amended to "boy," because the person in question was one of Garfield's students when he briefly worked as a teacher. Just remember that the next time you want to complain about school. If Garfield were your teacher, he would beat you up and laugh about it.

Laughing and punching jerks weren't the only things Garfield could multitask; he was our only ambidextrous president, and if you asked him a question, he could simultaneously write the answer down in Greek with one hand and Latin with the other, all while kicking you, if need be. That multitasking extended to everything— before he met his wife, Garfield dated three women *at the same time.*

As a workout, James Garfield would juggle Indian clubs. That sounds whimsical until you learn that Indian clubs are large bowling-pin-shaped pieces of wood that weigh fifty pounds each. Lifting weights wasn't enough; Garfield was only satisfied if his workout included the constant threat of having fifty-pound hunks of wood crash down onto his head. His strength and experience served him well in the Civil War, in which he was a major general (the youngest man to ever earn that title) and received praise from his superiors for his bravery.

Garfield wasn't *just* a fighter, he was also one of the smartest and most well read presidents we've ever had. He loved to meet with writers, engineers, and intellectuals and just sit quietly and learn from them. A senator from Massachusetts who knew Garfield in his twenties believed he could be a great success in science, math, English, public speaking, or the presidency. Most presidents follow a specific path—they start as either a lawyer or a war hero, move on to becoming a politician, and then become president. Garfield was a soldier *and* lawyer *and* politician *and* math and science whiz. This is only included in case it's humbling for you to know exactly how many ways Garfield is better than you—all at the same time.

Garfield made it to the presidency after serving nine straight terms in the House of Representatives. While his presidency was brief, he did manage to make a dent in the corrupt spoils system (which let people get government jobs by either paying for them or being friends with the right guy) that was still dominating politics. As soon as he was elected, he was hit by a storm of office seekers, corrupt jerks who wanted cushy, government jobs and power. Perhaps remembering the bullies who tried to push him around as a kid, Garfield would not be swayed and began working on the Pendleton Civil Service Act, which would legally require all federal government jobs to be awarded on the basis of merit and merit alone. This made Congress very angry, because they weren't used to dealing with a president who was quite this pushy, and also (okay, mostly) because it cut out a way for them to make money and wield power, but Garfield couldn't care less about what Congress wanted.

Garfield was an honest man and serious about reform. It's a shame that we'll never know how much of an impact he would have made on corruption, because his presidency was tragically cut short when a writer-turned-preacher-turned-lawyer-turned-lunatic named Charles Guiteau shot him twice in a train station. Guiteau believed that he was personally responsible for Garfield's presidential victory. Guiteau had, after all, delivered a speech in Garfield's favor to anyone who would listen (which, it turned out, wasn't very many people at all). Guiteau felt that since he got Garfield his job, it would only be fair of Garfield to return the favor and give Guiteau a job. Specifically, Guiteau thought he was entitled to an ambassadorship to France, and when the job didn't arrive at his doorstep, he felt betrayed. Guiteau believed that God spoke to him personally and ordered him to shoot Garfield, so he cornered Garfield as the president was about to board a train and gave him one last chance to appoint Guiteau ambassador to France. When Garfield refused to entertain the delusion, Guiteau shot him twice. This was back when the Secret Service only existed to chase down counterfeiters, by the way, so it was slightly easier for a crazy person like Guiteau to just walk up and shoot the president. After all, Garfield wasn't armed with a hickory cane like Andrew Jackson.

Amazingly, Garfield didn't die. He was taken to a hospital with one bullet still lodged in his body, which the doctors couldn't seem to find. In an effort to track the bullet down, doctors used a brand-new invention: the metal detector. The doctors would start cutting and digging whenever the device sensed metal. They did this several times, but they still couldn't find any trace of the bullet, even though they got the distinct impression that metal was present every single time. This was because the bed frame beneath Garfield was made of metal, but none of the doctors decided to check that. There was no time; they had a president to recklessly carve up and poke and prod with their filthy doctor fingers. One of the doctors accidentally punctured Garfield's liver, and another introduced streptococcus into his system, because for a long time "medicine" was just a bunch of guys messing around, often with unwashed hands. Garfield held out for eighty days before finally dying. As a neat epilogue to honor Garfield's legacy, reformers used his death to rally support for civil service reform. They held up Guiteau as an extreme example of patronage gone wild, and the country backed the movement, signaling the end of days for corrupt job seekers.

OFFICIAL FANTASY DREAM TEAM RATING

As one of the last truly tough presidents, Garfield might seem like a good fit for your **Brawn,** but he was clumsy and accident-prone. He accidentally chopped himself with an ax while doing chores as a child. And when he briefly worked on a ship, he fell overboard fourteen times in six weeks—pretty bold for someone who couldn't swim. His intelligence and passion for reform, however, make him a strong choice for **Moral Compass.**

THE PRESIDENTIAL ★ SCORECARD

? Brains
? Brawn
? Loose Cannon
? Moral Compass
? Roosevelt...

21

CHESTER A. ARTHUR

PRESIDENT SUPERVILLAIN

Presidential Term: 1881–1885

Political Party: Republican

Spouse: Ellen Herndon

Children: William, Chester Jr., and Ellen

Birthdate: October 5, 1829

Death Date: November 18, 1886

Fun Fact: According to a lot of people, Arthur was born in Canada and was thus ineligible to be president.

We've covered a lot of presidents who have done some crazy things (and—spoiler alert!—we're going to cover some *more* who do *even crazier* things), but at the end of the day, the men who have served our country were good people. Or at least they were doing what they thought was best. Some were misguided and some were corrupted by their friends, but they all genuinely seemed to at least *try* to help the country.

Only one president in this book was a supervillain (though Nixon was *also* evil, but in a unique and totally terrifying way). Ladies and gentlemen, meet Chester A. Arthur, the Lex Luthor of the American presidency.

To understand what kind of man Arthur was, we need to understand what America was like in the 1860s. For that, we need to understand political machines. The presidency was an obvious and showy position of power: everyone knew how influential and important the president was, and everyone saw the prestige that came with it. But some men, some dangerously ambitious men, saw a *similar* position in the 1800s—a position that also had a ton of power but received none of the scrutiny, none of the checks, and none of the balances presidents faced.

After the Civil War, the political conversation behind closed doors was less about the two established parties and more about the "political machines" that ran these parties. These machines picked candidates, provided the money to back candidates, and then either bought or stole elections. They were the power *behind* the power, and New York had the biggest and most controversial machine of all. For a long period in America's history, you simply couldn't be president without the support of one of these machines. Obviously, Arthur wanted to be part of the machine.

The U.S. Custom House in New York City was where the government collected tariffs, which are taxes on any goods that get imported into the United States, and it was run by just three officials. Each one was powerful, but one of these officials, the collector, was more powerful than the others. The collector was paid more money than almost every elected official (including the president of the United States). The collector had the power to hire whomever he wanted. And not just a small team; the average collector had power over one thousand jobs, and he had the ability to fire these people whenever he wanted, and there was absolutely nothing that they could do about it. The collector's employees were *dependent* on him, so they all jumped at the chance when he asked them for favors, almost always in the form of political contributions toward the campaign of whomever the U.S. Custom House decided to back that election. Because he had so much campaign money and a ton of potential campaign workers, presidential candidates were *also* fairly dependent on the collector. There was a lot of power, money, and prestige behind this position but very little accountability, and it always attracted the kind of people who wanted power more than anything else in life.

People vote, but the collector was one of the only people in history who could actually *make* someone president. So Chester A. Arthur wanted to be the collector.

To secure that job, Arthur made sure he was always making the right friends, shaking the right hands, and doing errands for the right party bosses (people who ran the political machines), many of which often involved breaking the law. Arthur did it, and he did it with a smile. Pick any random party boss from the mid- to late 1800s who, thanks to the watchful eye of history, has been exposed as a corrupt tinkerer in the big political machine, and I guarantee you'll find a quote from that boss praising Chester A. Arthur.

Arthur was spending so much time away from his family chasing this job that his wife, Ellen, fed up with the late nights and the time away from home, decided she was going to leave him in 1880. Before she got a chance to leave, though, she abruptly got sick and died.

Historical records show that pneumonia was the cause of death, and that's probably what happened. I'm not officially saying that Chester A. Arthur, like some cold-blooded, power-hungry monster, killed his own wife when she interfered

(this probably didn't happen)

with his plans, but I *am* pretending he did for the sake of making this chapter more interesting.

Eventually, after enough wheel greasing, glad-handing, and deal making, Arthur got his dream job. The Custom House was being investigated for corruption, accusations of patronage, and general awfulness, so the party bosses who relied on it wanted to hire someone who would seem honest and trustworthy to an outside observer to help them weather this investigative storm. Arthur was the natural choice.

Arthur did a great job. He sat at the top of the U.S. Custom House as collector, greasing the wheels of the political machine, fattening his own pockets with kickback after kickback, and dealing with the outside investigation the whole time. One investigation made it clear that Arthur forced an import company to pay a $270,000 fine (even though they were only *legally* required to pay $7,000), but even as these and other scandals surfaced, Arthur was reappointed by President Grant, because even the *president* was mostly powerless against the machines.

Well, not *all* presidents. Once Grant was gone, Rutherford B. Hayes stepped in and started reforming and stomping out the Custom House and other political machines. He personally fired Arthur, who retired in disgrace among scandal and corruption.

Oh, wait, no, he became president. Scratch that, he took a pay cut and power cut and *settled* for being president. First, he became the Republican nominee for vice president under James Garfield. No one would have thought that Arthur could have been a good vice president (he was a proven scoundrel), but he still got the job, because his ambition, as it always had, won out. It's important to note that he didn't want the vice presidency so he could do any real good; he wanted a position that commanded a great deal of respect but required very little work, and the vice presidency had that written all over it. John Adams, the first vice president in history, hated the job because it was a waste of time and carried no real responsibilities; no one *wants* that job, except Arthur, because of the *prestige*. So Arthur, more than anyone else in history, *campaigned* to be vice president. He again shook the right hands and smiled his big smile at the right people until he swooped in and took the nomination away from Garfield's first choice, a personal friend.

He did it in a single day. It all happened behind closed doors and with a lot of shady whispers and presumably slimy handshakes, so we'll never know exactly how Arthur, a proven con man, talked his way into the nomination; we just know that he did it in twenty-four hours.

Then Garfield was assassinated and Arthur—who, again, only became the vice president to cash a paycheck and get back the respect he lost in his disgraceful exit from his beloved collector position—was suddenly the president. Of the United States. *OF AMERICA!*

Now here is the craziest part. As president, Chester A. Arthur was *actually pretty decent.* He immediately started reforming the corrupt political-machine system—the one that had made him so powerful in the first place—launching a series of investigations and supporting a bunch of laws that would ultimately make these machines powerless. He signed into law the Pendleton Civil Service Act, one of the first major attempts at civil service reform. Under this act, you couldn't get a high-ranking government job just because your buddy *handed* it to you; you had to go through an official review process by a committee, something that was previously never done. It's the exact kind of law that, had it been around when he was a bit younger, would have kept Arthur from being the collector in the first place!

Arthur did a lot to fight corruption and did a ton for civil service reform. He's actually like a smarter, reformed Lex Luthor. The flaw of Lex Luthor and almost every other supervillain is *too* much of a craving for power and not knowing how to quit when ahead. If we made Luthor president, he'd just try to use that power to become president of the world, and then the universe, and he'd never stop until Superman stood up and took him down. Arthur, on the other hand, realized he was on top, so he quit while he was ahead and walked away ahead; he cashed in his chips and left the poker table. He covered his butt by defanging the corrupt people that could potentially manipulate him as president, and then he just walked away.

Arthur also worked diligently to repeal bans on Chinese immigrants and to break down tariffs, but otherwise his presidency was unremarkable. Neither of the two preceding presidents, Hayes and Garfield, had *really* made a clear and immediate impact on the country, so people didn't expect a whole lot out of their presidents around this time. Arthur reportedly stopped working every day around four o'clock, and when his term was coming to a close, he didn't seem interested in running again and his party didn't seem interested in supporting him anyway. He did some good and was ready to call it quits.

Even though his legacy as a president was mostly positive, never forget just how manipulative and devious Chester A. Arthur can be when he wants something. If Andrew Jackson was crazy because he drank too much of the "passion" part of the passion-ego-ambition cocktail all presidents drink, then Arthur is dangerous because he got drunk on ambition. He worked his way up in the political machine to get the position that carried the most power and pulled in the most money, and he used it for everything it was worth, down to the very last drop. When that no longer suited him, he set himself up in the vice presidency, because once he'd gotten a taste for privilege and respect, he wouldn't be satisfied with anything else. And then he became president, and as soon as he realized there was nothing else the political machines could do for him, he worked diligently to shut them down. He's cunning. He's wily. He's a supersmart supervillain whom I've (obviously) dubbed the Collector, and you need to watch your back around him.

OFFICIAL FANTASY DREAM TEAM RATING

A childhood friend of the twenty-first president of the United States told this story about Arthur: "When Chester was a boy, you might see him . . . watching the boys building a mud dam across the rivulet in the roadway. . . . Pretty soon, he would be ordering this one to bring stones, another sticks, and others sod and mud to finish the dam; and they would all do his bidding without question. But he took good care not to *get any of the dirt on his hand.*" That quote demonstrates a pretty good case for Arthur earning a spot as your **Brains,** but because he's *so* sneaky and untrustworthy (basically the opposite of the **Moral Compass**), I'd recommend keeping him on the bench.

CHA-
CLICK

22 AND 24

GROVER CLEVELAND

IS A SNEAKY BRICK WALL OF PAIN

Presidential Terms: 1885–1889 and 1893–1897
Political Party: Democratic
Spouse: Frances Folsom
Children: Ruth, Esther, Marion, Richard, and Francis
Birthdate: March 18, 1837
Death Date: June 24, 1908
Fun Fact: Cleveland is the only president to serve two nonconsecutive terms.
Also, his real first name was Stephen.

Stephen Grover Cleveland, our twenty-second president, wanted the world to know that he was a good and honest man. He held himself to a very high moral standard and he claimed to live by it, from the minute he was born until the minute he died. Literally. His last words were "I have tried so hard to do right."

Cleveland was a stern, efficient, no-nonsense type who believed in hard work. (According to his staff, it wouldn't be unusual to see Cleveland working until three or four in the morning, several nights in a row.) Character was important to Cleveland, a man who once said, "If we expect to become great and good men, and be respected and esteemed by our friends, we must improve our time when we are young." Was that from a campaign speech? Or in his inauguration? Nope. Cleveland said that when he was *nine years old,* and he never grew out of this line of thinking. You know what *I* said at nine years old? *Neither do I, because it was probably stupid.*

Cleveland's whole life is littered with stories of him going to great lengths to do what he thought was right, both personally and politically. While Cleveland was campaigning for the presidency, a woman he had casually dated before his marriage approached him with a son she claimed was his. Cleveland didn't know for sure that he was the father, but he still financially supported the child and checked up on him regularly because he believed it to be the right thing to do. As sheriff of Erie County, New York, he strongly opposed the death penalty and fought to outlaw it. He was unsuccessful, which was unfortunate for Cleveland (not to mention all those dudes who got the death penalty). When someone was sentenced to death, he *personally* performed the execution, which was almost unheard of. Executioners did exist, so there was no reason for the sheriff to personally deal out the death sentence, but Cleveland believed that upholding laws, even laws he personally hated, was important, and he wasn't going to force someone *else* to do it. This is a man with clarity of purpose.

Grover Cleveland made a good sheriff and a great politician, because in a time when political machines were sneakily making deals and wielding too much behind-the-scenes power, Cleveland stood tall as incorruptible. He never allowed himself to be seduced by office seekers and special-interest groups. "A public office is a public trust," Cleveland said, and that trust was sacred to him. Cleveland's goodness was superhuman. Biographer Allan Nevins said that "[h]e had no endowments that thousands of men do not have. He possessed honesty, courage, firmness, independence, and common sense. But he possessed them to a degree other men do not." Mark Twain said that Cleveland's character was on par with *Washington's*, and Mark Twain was a jerk to *everybody*.

That makes it all the more surprising to learn that one of the most shocking displays of presidential deception took place on Grover Cleveland's watch.

Record scratch!

During Cleveland's second term as president, a cancerous tumor was discovered in his mouth. This was right around the time when presidents started constantly being followed by the media. This happens today to presidents and plenty of other big politicians, but Cleveland was one of the first presidents to get this kind of treatment. (They followed Cleveland all the way to his honeymoon, much to his dismay.) Cleveland knew that he couldn't simply check into a hospital without the media taking notice, and he was concerned about the news getting out. He worried about the impact it might have on the national economy (which was already on fairly unstable ground). He worried about what the rest of the world would think if they saw America's president as weak or sick. (And presumably, he also worried about just, like, general cancer stuff.)

So the man who built his career around the image of total honesty and moral character staged a secret medical procedure. It was like an *Ocean's Eleven* heist, except instead of sending a ragtag team of specialists into a casino to steal a bunch of money, Cleveland sent a ragtag team of doctors and dentists into his mouth to steal a bunch of cancer.

He assembled his band of skilled and trustworthy specialists and scheduled a top-secret cancer heist/surgery. Oh, and to make sure the media didn't follow up, he arranged for the whole thing to take place *on a boat.* He told no one but the men performing his surgery, the ship's captain, and Daniel Lamont, his secretary of war. He didn't even tell his vice president, the man who would become the president should Cleveland die during his mysterious boat surgery.

On July 1, 1893, the president of the United States was sedated by nitrous oxide and ether, strapped into a chair anchored to the mast of a ship in the middle of the ocean, and underwent major surgery. Only about twelve people in the world knew about it; everyone else just thought the president was enjoying his Fourth of July weekend at sea (which, of course, is exactly what devious ole Cleveland *wanted* them to think). The already-risky surgery was made even more dangerous by being at sea, with the constant motion of the waves (which is why most doctors today rarely suggest getting mouth cancer surgery on a boat). The doctors cut into Cleveland's face and sinuses, making sure the incisions happened inside the president's mouth so as not to leave a visible scar, and removed a "gelatinous mound" of cancer. And, yeah, cancer comes in "gelatinous mounds," because *gross,* right?

The secret procedure was a success, and the public didn't even find out about it until decades later, nine years after Cleveland's death. Sure, the dentist who helped perform the surgery went public with the information as soon as it was clear the president was going to be in good health. He believed the danger had passed, but when he tried to share the story with the world, the White House aggressively and categorically denied his claims. The dentist was ridiculed and accused of being a liar.

GROVER'S 11

See, being president changes a man. It turned honest Grover Cleveland, a man who paid child support for a kid who probably wasn't even his, into a man who betrayed the public trust he claimed to hold so sacred. And we made him president *twice*!

Oh, right, twice! Here's a crazy thing. When the Clevelands were leaving the

White House in 1889, Cleveland's wife Frances told a staff member, "Now, Jerry, I want you to take good care of all the furniture and ornaments in the house, for I want to find everything just as it is now when we come back again." When asked when she would be back, Frances said, "Four years." She called her shot and claimed that Cleveland would be president again despite this never happening before in the history of presidents. It would seem like a completely outlandish and ridiculous prediction to make, and the fact that she was right is just bizarre. But she was. Cleveland came back, but before he could really dive into the presidency, the Panic of 1893 struck, thrusting America into an economic depression. It was largely out of his control (America was still arguing over whether our money would be "greenbacks" [traditional money] or backed by silver), but presiding over the Panic was one of the few things for which Cleveland is remembered today.

Which is unfair, because he was just a rad, tough dude. As a child, he wasn't just talking eloquently about how "to become great"; he was also regularly ripping fence posts out of the ground with his bare hands. He was five feet eleven inches and two hundred fifty pounds of president, and his fists were described as "ham-like," which might be delicious but is probably just scary and painful. He loved hunting and often carried around a rifle nicknamed Death and Destruction, which isn't a nickname a rifle earns for being *pretty*.

OFFICIAL FANTASY DREAM TEAM RATING

As big and as armed as he was, Cleveland wasn't so tough that he'd be a good fit for your **Brawn** (he reportedly loathed exercise and most bodily movement in general), but he might be worth considering for your **Brains.** It's not *everyone* who can fool the entire nation and pull off the *mouth cancer heist of the century*.

BENJAMIN HARRISON

THE HUMAN ICEBERG

Presidential Term: 1889–1893
Political Party: Republican
Spouses: Caroline Scott and Mary Scott Lord
Children: Russell and Mary with his wife Caroline, and Elizabeth with his wife Mary
Birthdate: August 20, 1833
Death Date: March 13, 1901
Fun Fact: Harrison was the last president to wear a beard (so far).

Benjamin Harrison is not to be messed with. He was quick, stocky, and efficient with his actions, and according to historian William DeGregorio, he "tackled problems through mastery of detail." Harrison was a man who was completely immovable when convinced of his own rightness. (This, combined with his cold nature, earned him the nickname the Human Iceberg, though I also have a pet theory that it's because he single-handedly sunk the *Titanic* with a head butt.) Harrison's rigid and stern nature (he was described by Theodore Roosevelt as "cold-blooded") applied to his schoolyard fights, his politics, and everything else in his life.

Unfortunately for anyone who has ever come up against him, Harrison was *always* convinced of his own rightness, thanks to his deep and personal relationship with religion. A devout Presbyterian, Harrison was a former deacon and Sunday school teacher, and as president, he was so serious about his religion that he conducted no political business on Sundays. When he won the election, the first words out of his mouth were, "Now I walk with God."

You want to know the most terrifying kind of person? It's the guy with a military background having absolute power who sincerely believes he was elected as God's friend. That's a confidence that's almost impossible to match. It was also a huge leap, because there's some compelling evidence that Harrison's win wasn't exactly legitimate. You see, despite the best efforts of Arthur and Cleveland and the other reformer presidents, some party bosses still had a little bit of power, and the ones who did *hated* President Cleveland for his honesty. Harrison lost the popular vote to Cleveland and only won the electoral votes from New York (Cleveland's home state) because of the party bosses who ran New York. The bosses wanted to punish Cleveland, so they got together, raised some money, and (possibly) stole the election for Harrison. (When Harrison credited his victory to God in front of Matthew Quay, one of the bosses who ensured victory, Quay reportedly said, "Then let God reelect you" before storming out of the president's sight.) Even though all evidence was pointing toward shady corruption, Harrison wanted to believe that God made him president, and nothing was going to shake him of that belief.

That's not to say that Harrison's supreme self-confidence was *completely* misguided. In 1862, Harrison raised the 70th Indiana Infantry and served as their colonel in the Civil War. Even though he had no military experience at the time, the governor of Indiana had to beg him *twice* to become a colonel for the Infantry, because he simply radiated the kind of butt-kicking toughness that you look for in a colonel. Harrison eventually accepted his command position, and even though he was a strict disciplinarian (he accepted only the best from himself and therefore wouldn't tolerate anything less from anyone else), he earned the admiration of the soldiers he commanded with his bravery and courage. While he later admitted to not enjoying the war (he claimed he'd prefer to have breakfast instead of a fight, which, sure, if *those* are your choices, obviously), he was just as thorough and calculating on the battlefield as he was anywhere else, and just as uncompromising.

Harrison was a real standout as president. He took office during a period of reform, when presidents like Cleveland and Arthur and Hayes (and even Garfield with his limited term) were focused on stomping out domestic corruption and working to earn back the trust of the American people. These were noble endeavors to be sure, but they weren't exactly *exciting* to the average person. No one was going to war and no one was making big, grand speeches or freeing slaves or declaring independence; they were all just quietly trying to tidy up America. Harrison, on the other hand, embodied the kind of "America as global bully" stereotype that other presidents before and since always tried to downplay. While his predecessors seemed passive, Harrison was taking *action*. Harrison wanted America to be *bigger* (he added North and South Dakota, Montana, Washington, Idaho, and Wyoming to the Union), he wanted it to be *stronger* (he spent money building up the navy and strengthening our military), and he wanted the rest of the world to recognize and fear the amazing and beautiful country that was America. When Canadian ships started fishing in areas that Harrison believed belonged to America, he had the ships and the crews taken prisoner. When he saw Hawaii, he thought, *I want that,* and sent in American troops to overthrow the Hawaiian queen in a coup. Remember, Harrison was a man who believed he was right *and* God's buddy, so if he wanted your ships or your tropical island paradise, he was going to *take it.*

When Harrison couldn't get as much done in America as he'd wanted, he turned outward to the rest of the world to leave his mark. Harrison's intense patriotism (a good quality to have in a president) and bullish toughness (a *terrifying* one) meant that he would never back down from a fight, especially if it involved another country. During his presidency, two American sailors got into a fight and died in a saloon brawl in Valparaíso, Chile. It wasn't an act of aggression from Chile as a nation; it was just a saloon fight. Still, Harrison told the Chilean minister of foreign affairs that if Chile didn't immediately and publicly apologize and pay some form of restitution for the two deceased sailors, *he would go to war.* The minister eventually apologized and paid $75,000, because the guy who threatens to send his constantly expanding navy to war after the accidental deaths of two men is *not* a man you try to reason with. Later, the roles were reversed—a number of Italian immigrants were lynched in New Orleans, and Italy's prime minister similarly demanded an apology. Harrison refused to apologize, accused Italy of overreacting on the basis of absolutely nothing, and threatened *them* with war. No one messes with America on Harrison's watch, not even people who aren't technically trying to mess with America.

Harrison isn't just eager to start a fight; he also knows how to win one. Late one night, a deranged man broke into the White House through a window with a belly full of liquor and a strong desire to kill President Harrison. The attacker was able to subdue the *two men* who tried to take him down. Two doormen tried to double-team the invading drunk, but they were simply no match for his passion and whiskey punches. Harrison, who got out of bed and moved to action as soon as he heard a window break, burst into the room with the drunk lunatic and single-handedly took him down, pinning his arms at his sides so hard that one of the doormen likened Harrison's grip to that of a vise. With the man still pinned motionless, Harrison calmly asked the two White House staffers what else he could do for them, and one sheepishly replied that he could maybe cut down one of the window cords and use it to tie the intruder up. Harrison did it quickly and then handed the man over to the police. He didn't do this as some young spring chicken in the war, but as a crotchety, bearded president in his late fifties.

He continued aggressively trying to make America the best, creating national parks and starting free mail delivery. Further, Harrison secured millions of dollars to be paid to Union veterans of the Civil War. Harrison's decision *not* to set aside money for Confederate veterans, in addition to his attempts to protect black voters, alienated the South and gave his opponents all the ammunition they needed to defeat him when he ran for reelection. On March 4, 1893, Grover Cleveland was *again* the president, making Harrison the bearded, icy meat in the middle of a Cleveland sandwich. (Harrison is so far the only president to earn this distinction.)

OFFICIAL FANTASY DREAM TEAM RATING

If Harrison's right and God really *is* his buddy, he's probably your best choice for the **Moral Compass.** He's as tough as any of our other tough-guy presidents, so he'd be a natural fit for the **Brawn** as well.

25

WILLIAM MCKINLEY'S

GOT FLOWER POWER

Presidential Term: 1897–1901

Political Party: Republican

Spouse: Ida Saxton

Children: Katherine and Ida

Birthdate: January 29, 1843

Death Date: September 14, 1901

Fun Fact: Instead of traveling for his campaign, McKinley spoke to over 700,000 people from his front porch. His opponent, William Jennings Bryan, who traveled all over the country making grand speeches, lost by a landslide.

William "The Major" McKinley was a man's man. He smoked cigars, like a lot of presidents, but he also straight-up *ate them,* like *no one.*

McKinley volunteered for service in the Civil War at eighteen years old. At the time, he was weak and sickly and had no combat or fighting experience, so he was put to work in the commissary. The kitchen might not seem like the most exciting place to be in a war, but McKinley made it work; he earned distinction and respect for running right to the front lines to make sure all the soldiers had food and water, taking enemy fire the whole time. He regularly wrote in his diary that he knew he would probably die soon, but he wasn't nervous or afraid because he was serving his country (and literally serving his countrymen) and would die doing what he believed in. McKinley was so good at feeding people and not dying that he was quickly promoted several times, eventually earning the rank and nickname the Major. His commander, Rutherford B. Hayes, said that McKinley showed "unusual and unsurpassed capacity." He entered the army weak and pale, but he left after four years looking strong, healthy, and confident.

As a man and a president, McKinley never made any decisions without carefully thinking through every issue from every angle. During his presidency, there was a lot of pressure from his own cabinet and from sensationalist journalists like Joseph Pulitzer and William Randolph Hearst to get America involved in Cuba's war for independence from Spain. Hearst and Pulitzer worked Americans into a frenzy with their ridiculous and exaggerated tales of Spanish savagery, and it seemed like everyone in the country was begging for war, but McKinley wouldn't be moved by newspapermen. He had already lived through a war, he'd seen bodies pile up, and he treated military aggression like an absolute last resort. Critics unfairly accused McKinley of suffering from indecision, but really he was just thoughtful. He only got America involved in the war after he'd exhausted every available diplomatic solution, and when he *did* get us involved, he *really* committed.

McKinley went from being against the Spanish-American War to being an incredibly competent and decisive wartime commander in chief. He converted a room of the White House into a war room and was directly connected to just about every commander in the field, personally checking in with soldiers by phone several times a day. This strategic war room was unprecedented for a president, but McKinley felt right at home. His mastery of detail and his military experience made him an incredibly efficient commander, and the Spanish-American War ended in just four months with more American casualties happening as a result of disease than actual attacks. It was an important war, because it established America as a global superpower and got Northerners, Southerners, blacks, and whites all fighting together for a noble cause (something Americans, who were still dealing with the aftermath of the Civil War, desperately needed to see). America even got control of the Philippines after the war and *we didn't even want it.*

Don't let the battle mastery and cigar chompery fool you; McKinley was also just a *super* nice and likable guy. He was polite, gave everyone the benefit of the doubt, and charmed Democrats and Republicans alike. Plus he was just the greatest husband ever. McKinley's devotion to his wife was legendary in Washington. When he was governor, McKinley made sure that his office was across the street from his home. This was because every single day at three o'clock, it was important for him to stop what he was doing, go to his window, and give his wife, Ida, a simple wave. (She would stand in the window of their home and wave back.) Even though they had breakfast together every morning, and even though he *also* waved to her from across the street right before he entered his office.

As president, McKinley broke protocol by having his wife sit next to him during official White House dinners. (It was customary at the time for the president's wife to sit with the guest of honor, ACROSS from, but not next to, the president.) He did this because Ida had epilepsy and was prone to seizures, and if he sensed

one coming on during dinner, he would cover Ida's face with a napkin or cloth to spare her the embarrassment of having people watch her face twitch and contort. When the attack passed, he'd remove the napkin and move on as if nothing had happened. *Super* sweet guy.

McKinley wore a red carnation every day as a good-luck charm, and because it pleased his wife. You can say whatever you want about luck, but we have no evidence to suggest that the carnation *wasn't* magically infused with luck. Minutes after he removed his lucky carnation and gave it to a young girl as a present, he was shot by a deranged anarchist (a person who doesn't believe the government or *any* ruling body should be in charge, and that people should be able to govern themselves) named Leon Czolgosz. Being shot didn't ruin McKinley's reputation as a nice guy—his first words after being shot were "Don't let them hurt him" (upon seeing his assassin tackled to the ground) and "My wife, be careful . . . how you tell her, oh, be careful!" His immediate concern was for his assailant and his wife, and how she would take the news of his attack.

His kindness was not rewarded. When McKinley got to the hospital, the only doctor around who could perform surgery was a gynecologist who couldn't find the bullet. Despite the doctor's best efforts, McKinley died on September 14, 1901, nine days after being shot.

OFFICIAL FANTASY DREAM TEAM RATING

McKinley's sort of the total package and would be a good fit for any role other than the **Loose Cannon.** (He's way too thoughtful and measured for that.) Otherwise you can't go wrong sticking him in any position.

26

THEODORE ROOSEVELT

IS THE BEST

Presidential Term: 1901–1909
Political Party: Republican and Bull Moose
Spouses: Alice Lee and Edith Carow
Children: Alice with his wife Alice, Theodore III, Kermit, Ethel, Archibald, and Quentin with his wife Edith
Birthdate: October 27, 1858
Death Date: January 6, 1919
Fun Fact: Read the chapter title. TR is the best.

It's hard to imagine that Theodore Roosevelt, without question the toughest president we have ever had or will ever have, was once sickly. Indeed, throughout his childhood, he was almost always on the verge of death. He complained of stomachaches, headaches, and asthma and wrote in his journal that "nobody seemed to think [he] would live." When most kids are as perpetually sick as Roosevelt was, they get babied by their parents, but TR's folks knew they were raising a steel-chomping cowboy-in-training, and they treated him as such from day one. When Teedie's (his family's nickname for him) asthma acted up, his father gave him a cigar to smoke and his mother rubbed his chest so hard that he spit up blood. Roosevelt's father, who wanted TR to toughen up, told him on his fourteenth birthday that he had "the mind but . . . not the body, and without the help of the body, the mind cannot go as far as it should." TR simply said, "I'll make my body."

And boy, oh boy. He did.

TR took up boxing. And wrestling. And hunting. And running. And fighting. Gradually, he beat his sickness, even his asthma, making him the only human in history to intimidate asthma into submission (though, really, can you blame the asthma?). TR wasn't satisfied with just getting stronger and overcoming his illnesses; he wanted to beat everything. He consciously forced himself to take whatever path seemed harshest and most dangerous, surrounding himself with whatever inspired the most terror (*like Batman, you guys*).

TR summed up his life philosophy and his fear-immersive approach to life simply, that "man does in fact become fearless by sheer dint of practicing fearlessness." That, ladies and gentlemen, is the most Rooseveltian sentence ever written.

Going through Roosevelt's résumé is like reading a how-to guide on manliness. He was a cattle rancher, a deputy sheriff, an explorer, a police commissioner, the assistant secretary of the navy, the governor of New York, and a war hero. Also, a full-on cowboy. Tragedy struck when TR's mother and wife died on the exact same day, and while some people take a blow like that and just lock themselves up in a room and cry for days, Teddy, like the Batman that he was, left his home behind and moved out to a wild and untamed area. Eventually TR would return and marry Edith Carow, making a giant Rooseveltian family of champions, but before all that he had some grieving to do. In TR's case, this meant going West to work as a cowboy—catching, riding, and branding horses and bulls and occasionally beating some bullies who got out of line. *We* know TR as the tough adventurer, but it's easy to forget that he was born into the New York aristocracy. He loved nature, adventure, and the outdoors, but up until this point had never really had to *rough it*. When he went out West, he immediately stuck out with his glasses, his fancy East Coast accent, and his inexperience. Roosevelt was raised by very wealthy parents who spent a lot of time attending parties with other wealthy families and giving away some of their money to help others. His father helped found the Metropolitan Museum of Art, for crying out loud. To the outlaws, cowboys, and punks there, TR was just some elitist city boy. One night TR was tired after a long day of cowboying, so he entered a saloon to have a drink and catch some rest. An unruly cowboy (with a cocked gun in each hand) made fun of TR, calling him Four Eyes and demanding that he buy everyone in the saloon a drink. TR tried ignoring him, but when the cowboy persisted, TR gave the armed moron three quick punches to the face. The man was knocked unconscious, and as soon as he woke up the next morning, he left town, never to be seen again, because maybe he never stopped running. Well, no one would confuse TR for some fancy city boy ever again. This instantly established him as someone not to be messed with. In the Western land of outlaws and cowboys, TR was *still* the toughest.

On another occasion, TR was fox hunting with some friends and almost *everyone* had some kind of accident. (Fox hunting used to be CRAZY dangerous.) One man dislocated his knee; another broke several ribs; another got half of his face ripped off by what must have been the angriest fox in the forest; and TR himself got knocked to the ground, landed on a pile of stones, and then got crushed by his own horse. His face was covered with blood and his left wrist was fractured, but he got back on the horse and continued to ride and hunt for five miles. The next day he went for a three-hour walk.

Out of all his jobs, hobbies, and passions, Roosevelt always had a special place in his heart for unadulterated violence. He talked about fighting the way poets talked about love, saying once that every man "who has in him any real power to joy in battle knows that he feels it when the wolf begins to rise in his heart; he does not then shrink from blood or sweat or deem that they mar the fight; he revels in them, in the toil, the pain, and the danger, as but setting off the triumph."

Roosevelt was always praying for a chance to serve in a war, and in 1898, TR got his wish when America intervened in a dispute between Spain and Cuba. Roosevelt quickly formed the 1st United States Volunteer Cavalry, a group of cowboys and fighters referred to as the Rough Riders. They were one of the first groups in the war, all because Roosevelt pushed them hard, saying "It will be awful if we miss the fun" (because Roosevelt and I have very different ideas of fun). Most people already know of the Rough Riders and their historic charge up San Juan Hill, but few know that since their horses had to be left behind, the Riders made this charge entirely on foot. Whenever it looked like someone might retreat, Roosevelt threatened to shoot them, warning that he always kept his promises. Most of his troops laughed, saying, *"Ha ha, that's true,"* and continued fighting, all laughing together about how crazy Roosevelt was.

Don't think that Roosevelt lost his obsession with violence when he became president. Don't you dare *ever* think that. TR strolled through the White House with a pistol on his person at all times, though with his black belt in jujitsu and his history as a champion boxer, it wasn't like he really needed it. It wasn't just his war record or that he knew several different ways to kill a person that made Roosevelt such a cool guy. It wasn't even that he kept a bear and a lion at the White House as pets (though that certainly helps). Teddy Roosevelt was a man of the people. He received letters from cavalrymen complaining about having to ride twenty-five miles a day for training, and in response, Teddy rode horseback for one hundred miles, from sunrise to sunset, at fifty-one years old, *while president,* effectively removing anyone's right to complain about anything ever again.

Roosevelt handpicked William Howard Taft to be his successor when he left the White House, but he was so disappointed with the way Taft ran things that he invented a new party—the Bull Moose Party—and attempted to run for a third term against Taft when he ran for reelection in 1912. The Democrats ended up winning that election because Roosevelt divided the Republican Party; some wanted to support Roosevelt, the hero, but others wanted to stick with Taft to keep Republicans in the White House. As a result, neither got enough votes and the Democrats won easily.

Roosevelt was never injured in any of the battles he fought, but while he was campaigning for that third term, TR was shot by a madman. Instead of treating the wound, Roosevelt delivered his campaign speech with the bleeding, undressed bullet hole in his chest. Even though he said he would take it easy on this speech given the circumstances, he spoke for *an hour and a half.* Right before addressing the crowd, Roosevelt opened his coat, revealed the bleeding wound, and said, "The bullet is in me now."

Upon leaving the White House, some presidents returned to law, enjoyed retirement peacefully, or wrote books. Roosevelt went on African safaris and hunted big game, then went on a South American expedition and almost died in the process. TR, his son Kermit, and eighteen others were supposed to take a fairly standard boat ride up the Amazon River when TR changed his mind at the last second and demanded a more challenging trip. Their guide suggested they go to the "River of Doubt," an uncharted and extremely dangerous trip full of vipers, anacondas, piranhas, jaguars, and natives armed with poison darts. The group had gone only a quarter of the way down the river and were already in pretty bad shape, between diseases, starvation, and exhaustion. Roosevelt cut his leg and nearly died from the infection. He drifted in and out of consciousness and told his crew to leave him behind and just let him die so he wouldn't slow them down, but no one in a million years would leave a wounded Roosevelt behind. Eventually, they ran into some locals who knew the river well. The locals helped the crew down the river, where they met a relief party their guide had previously set up. It was here, after being on the River of Doubt for over two months, that Roosevelt received medical attention from a local doctor and lived to tell the story of one of the most insane postpresidential journeys of all time.

The River of Doubt was renamed Rio Roosevelt, because Roosevelt *is the best.*

OFFICIAL FANTASY DREAM TEAM RATING

Roosevelt Roosevelt Roosevelt! He's perfect for literally every position. The warrior-politician with the soul of a poet. I love this guy so much. *Rooooooooosevelt!*

27

WILLIAM HOWARD TAFT

NEVER EVEN WANTED *TO BE PRESIDENT*

Presidential Term: 1909–1913
Political Party: Republican
Spouse: Helen "Nellie" Herron
Children: Robert, Helen, and Charles
Birthdate: September 15, 1857
Death Date: March 8, 1930
Fun Fact: Taft was the first president to openly take up golf,
which caused an enormous golf boom in America.

Maxing out at three hundred forty pounds, William Howard Taft has the distinction of being not only our fattest president, which is one of two things he's known for. (The other involves a bathtub, which I'll discuss later, and it's *hilarious*.)

Taft's presidency is mostly (unfortunately) remembered for how average it was. He followed Teddy Roosevelt, and even though Taft's big, giant feet could literally squash Roosevelt's shoes, Taft was never really a big-enough man to fill them. Roosevelt believed the president could and should do anything he wanted (unless the law explicitly said not to), and Taft thought the president could *only* do what was explicitly written in the Constitution. As a result, Taft's administration was full of a lot of important reforms, but it lost the excitement of Roosevelt's time in office. And Taft's staunch, by-the-book attitude angered Roosevelt so much that he decided to run against Taft in the next election, which almost ripped the Republican Party apart completely and caused them both to lose.

Did this upset Taft? Not really. In a lot of ways, Taft was one of the saner men to serve as president because, unlike almost everyone else in this book, he really, *really* didn't want to be president. Taft loved the law and wanted to be a chief justice of the Supreme Court. He only accepted the presidential nomination in the first place for two reasons: (1) his ambitious wife, Nellie, wanted him to, and (2) Teddy Roosevelt had handpicked Taft as his successor, and Taft honestly didn't know the polite way to turn the offer down. I've mentioned before that one of the main things all presidents shared was a strong sense of ambition. Taft didn't have that drive himself, so Nellie supplied all of it. Seventeen-year-old Nellie visited the White House in 1877 as a guest of President Hayes, and she instantly decided that she needed to live in the White House one day as First Lady. She studied politics and the law and sought to marry a man who she thought could be president and encourage all her intellectual pursuits. Taft was just such a man. When Taft was working in Washington as solicitor general, it was Nellie who went out networking and strengthening Taft's political chances by meeting the right people and making the right connections. She even regularly wrote letters to and held meetings with President Roosevelt, urging him to support Taft. *Roosevelt!* Talk about courage.

As First Lady, Nellie made important changes to the White House staff. (She made sure black Americans were hired to be White House ushers, a previously all-white position that came with a lot of status.) She went on a tour of federal buildings, put together a report on the working conditions (mostly for women), and was instrumental in getting Executive Order 1498 passed, which improved sanitation and safety conditions in all executive buildings. This was the first time in history that a First Lady managed to successfully propose a federal act. If we had to do it over again, we probably should have just elected Nellie.

Taft wasn't exactly a do-nothing president; he really got rid of some dead weight in the Treasury Department, trimmed a lot of fat out of the military budget, and busted a lot of bloated trusts. In fact, the only time he broke a reduction-related promise was when he vowed to the American people that he'd lose thirty pounds while in the White House. (He actually *gained* fifty over four years.)

Taft *really* shined in his postpresidency career, when Warren G. Harding named him chief justice of the Supreme Court. Taft remains the only person in history to serve as both president and chief justice, and Taft considered this judicial role to be the highlight of his life. Taft didn't look back fondly on his presidency according to letters he wrote to close friends. He hardly even remembered his time spent in the White House.

This is largely because Taft *didn't* spend too much time in the White House. He hated the job so much that he spent most of his time driving around, golfing, or just generally avoiding being the president. He was always a big guy, but he tended to overeat when he got into the White House because he was sad and food seemed to cheer him up. As soon as he left office, he lost eighty pounds and was happier and healthier than he'd been since college. Before he'd even lost his reelection bid in 1912, he'd already confessed that he had his eyes on the future.

With all that weight, you can bet that Taft was a pretty tough guy. He was Yale's intramural heavyweight wrestling champion and *also* graduated second in his class. *From Yale!* That's all impressive, but hey, I promised you a story involving a bathtub, so let's really get to it. William Howard Taft, an adult man, *while president,* once got stuck in a bathtub.

It's one of my all-time favorite stories about presidents and my number one favorite story about bathtubs. One day, after packing on his presidential pounds, Taft actually got stuck in the White House tub while taking a bath. He sat there for a while stewing, not only in his own considerable juices, but also in the knowledge that no matter what he did as president or a Supreme Court judge, *this* was what he'd be remembered for. He could make significant contributions to his country, but at the end of the day, jerks who write books about presidents would still dedicate the bulk of their Taft chapters to this one stupid, hilarious story.

Taft struggled to wriggle himself free of the tub's clutches, but he knew it was no use. Finally, having abandoned the idea that maybe he could just live in the bathtub forever, Taft called to an aide to help him out. The aide, who recognized immediately that this wasn't a job for one man, called three of his buddies and the team got Taft out. Four men. It took four men to extract the president of the United States from his tub. A new tub was then installed just to accommodate the extra-large president.

Even outside the tub, Taft's overeating was a problem, as it led to issues of flatulence and gas. He would embarrass his staff by burping and farting too much in front of visiting foreign dignitaries, and if that's not bad enough, you're lying, because that's TOTALLY bad enough. Taft would eat so much that he'd pass out in

the middle of meetings and conversations. This is less about Taft being a slob and more about him being really depressed in the role of president. The man who once wrote "Politics make me sick" meant it literally.

OFFICIAL FANTASY DREAM TEAM RATING

You could bring Taft on as your **Brains,** but only on the condition that he bring Nellie and let her make all the decisions.

28

WOODROW WILSON

THE HALF-DEAD PRESIDENT

Presidential Term: 1913–1921
Political Party: Democratic
Spouses: Ellen Axson and Edith Bolling
Children: Margaret, Jessie, and Eleanor
Birthdate: December 28, 1856
Death Date: February 3, 1924
Fun Fact: Wilson was the first president to hold a press conference.

Thomas Woodrow Wilson is the only person in history to have a PhD *and* the presidency *and* a Nobel Peace Prize under his belt. He was also dyslexic, blind in one eye, and unable to read until age ten, which should tell you the most important lesson you need to learn about Wilson: if he wants something, he's going to go for it. In his first term alone, he made more reforms and had more laws passed than almost any other president before or since, including child labor laws. It was on his watch that women were given the right to vote and workers were given the right to not work so many hours in a single day that they die.

The other important lesson you need to learn about Wilson is that he was just a walking sack of death. In addition to the previously mentioned partial blindness, he also suffered constant, crushing headaches that never went away and lived with recurring stomach pain so bad that he traveled with his own stomach pump. He used the stomach pump on himself every day at the suggestion of a second-rate physician until a White House doctor said, *"Who told you to do that? HOLY COW! STOP THAT."* He had writer's cramp in his right hand and stabbing pains in his left shoulder and leg, and he lived through several strokes, which damaged his brain.

His already shaky health was tested even more in his second term. Wilson proudly kept America out of World War I in his first term. (He was so proud of this that his campaign slogan for his second term was "He Kept Us Out of War.") But when Germany refused to stop attacking American ships, Wilson was forced to declare war and drop the hammer. And drop it he did! Wilson led us into war during his second term, made sure our soldiers always had food and ammunition, and signed a peace treaty before his term ended. Seeing peace even in war, Wilson thought of World War I as an opportunity to build the League of Nations, an international superfriends team focused on maintaining global peace *by any means necessary* (diplomacy, usually). At the time, no one else agreed with Wilson's idea, and the lack of support just seemed to make Wilson sicker and crazier. Oh, right, the craziness. Wilson was, by his own description, "impulsive, passionate . . . , canny, tenacious, [and] cold," and he once "compared himself to a dormant volcano, placid on the outside, a boiling caldron within." When he pitched his League of Nations to the world, only to get laughed at, the lava he kept stored on the inside started to bubble to the surface. He became angry and rude and bitter, and his body started falling apart in a really bizarre way. Wilson's body started morphing so that his appearance began to match his inner anger/craziness. The strain of having to deal with uncooperative foreign allies "contracted [Wilson's] usually relaxed facial muscles into sharp ridges of hostility," making him appear "haggard"; he perpetually looked angry and ferocious. Also, that one blind eye started twitching and fluttering like a tiny, round humming bird trapped in an angry volcano face.

During this time, Wilson grew suspicious of even his closest friends (something historians later attributed to undiagnosed brain damage). He went days without sleeping and his brain slowly started deteriorating, which, like everything at this point, only made Wilson angrier and more stubborn. Determined to win public support for the League of Nations, Wilson decided to go against the orders of his wife, doctors, and basic common sense, and toured the country to give speeches that would rally people to his side. He rode all over America, coughing and sneezing and being fed predigested foods (the only foods he could eat) by day, and giving rousing speeches by night (sometimes five in one day). He delivered his speeches with closed eyes, shaking hands, and a weakened voice. With his wheezing, sleeplessness, strained mumbling, rapidly failing body, and singular, obsessed focus, it's not completely uncalled for to label Woodrow Wilson our first zombie president.

After his first stroke, which left him paralyzed on his left side, Wilson cut the tour short and went back to the White House to relax, because presidenting is such a cakewalk of a job that we should all do it when we need a vacation.

Here was the problem: the doctors believed that if Wilson stepped down and left the White House, the disgrace and humiliation would kill him. Wilson's health had gotten so bad that he could barely walk; his mind was deteriorating so thoroughly that he could barely make decisions; and his aides started to resign, one by one, having grown tired of the president's hurtful outbursts and personal attacks.

So . . . who was actually running things?

Here's a crazy thing: in 1919, Wilson's second wife, Edith, became the unofficial president of the United States. Edith, a direct descendant of Pocahontas (!!), decided which matters would be brought to Wilson and which ones would be thrown out. While she claims she never made a single executive decision, she has

admitted to deciding what was important and what was not after reading every paper from every senator or secretary. Her presidential takeover was kept far out of the public eye. (People back then, as they are today, were very much against the idea of a mummy—or his wife—being president.) She convinced the press that Wilson hadn't suffered a stroke and was instead just "tired." For a number of months of Wilson's presidency, no one was allowed to speak to the president without going through Edith first. It could be argued that Edith was our first female president, even though no one voted for her and she called her tenure running the White House a stewardship.

Wilson (and Edith) did a lot of good for America, but he also earns a distinction for being one of our country's most racist presidents, and he wasn't even one of the presidents who personally owned slaves. Most of *those* guys were *less racist* than Wilson. Wilson sought to decrease the amount of black people in office and even segregated federal government offices, something that hadn't been done since the mid-1800s. It could be argued that Wilson was from a different time, but it could *also* be argued that *so was Lincoln, you racist jerk.*

OFFICIAL FANTASY DREAM TEAM RATING

A physically weak racist with rapidly failing health? Wilson can sit this one out.

29

WARREN G. HARDING

IS DESPERATE TO PROVE HE'S GOOD AT SOMETHING

Presidential Term: 1921–1923
Political Party: Republican
Spouse: Florence Kling
Children: None
Birthdate: November 2, 1865
Death Date: August 2, 1923
Fun Fact: Harding was elected by the largest popular majority in history despite being truly terrible as president.

Historians often like to point out how easy it is to ridicule the twenty-ninth president of the United States, Warren G. Harding, for his spectacular failures as a pathetic worm of a president. But they neglect to mention that it's also incredibly fun and very justified. Harding is one of the most consistently hated presidents in the history of politics. Enemies, friends, family members, and voters walked all over Harding throughout his life, and every time, he just *took* it, sitting idly by while members of his cabinet royally ripped off America in scandal after scandal. The first time he tried to speak in front of a large gathering of Republicans, his own party *booed him*. Teddy Roosevelt's daughter called him a slob *for no clear reason*. His miserable presidency was full of bad decisions, followed by endless criticism, and he just took it all with a smile and a *"Thank you, sir, may I have another?"*

The only president who ranks lower than Harding on any poll is William Henry Harrison, and that's because Harrison died thirty days into his term. All Harding had to do to be better was live slightly longer, which he did, but that was *it*. He was lazy and gave cushy government jobs to all his longtime friends, who used their positions to illegally make massive amounts of money off the trust of the American people. He turned the White House into a frat house, bringing in a bunch of pals who would smoke, gamble, drink, and figure out new and creative ways to rob the American people. He made his friend Albert Fall the secretary of the interior, who was later arrested for accepting bribes in exchange for leasing American oil fields to personal business associates. This came to be known as the Teapot Dome Scandal, and while it was the most famous of the scandals to rock the Harding administration, it wasn't the *only* one. The head of the Office of Alien Property Custodian ("Alien" meaning "foreign enemy," not the kind from space) *and* even the head of the Department of Justice were *also* convicted of accepting bribes, and the head of the Veterans Bureau stole profits and organized a small underground drug ring (which, yes, is a *supervillainesque* level of evil).

Don't confuse Harding's ineptitude as a political leader with a lifetime of cowardice or stupidity. Harding, for all his many faults, was very calculating and *sneaky*. He liked to put up a front as a softy and a gentleman while secretly getting what he wanted, as he did in 1884 when he bought the *Marion Daily Star,* a sinking ship of a newspaper in Ohio with only seven hundred subscribers. With Harding at the helm, the *Star* quickly surpassed its competitors. Some people believed the paper's success came from shrewd business practices, or the goodwill Harding had built up in the community, but Harding's charm and likability were just a distraction. The *Star* succeeded because Harding trashed the name of his paper's biggest competitor, the *Marion Independent.* Harding always *seemed* to genuinely like all people, which is why it came as such a shock when his newspaper started accusing the competing *Independent*'s owner "with being 'a liar,' 'a lickspittle,' and 'a moral leper.'"

Whether or not the owner was, in fact, "a lickspittle," and whether or not such a word was ever even a thing, is all lost to history. The bottom line is that it worked, and the *Independent* collapsed under the might of the tough-as-nails *Star.* Harding later used the influence of his paper to launch his political career and attract the attention of the Republican Party.

As a politician, Harding didn't really have any passionate beliefs or policies. He just *wanted* the presidency so badly; it didn't matter what he had to say or do to get there. He had a track record for voting for what he thought was going to *win,* regardless of whether he thought he was voting for the *right* side. It wasn't about morals; it was about backing the right horse to avoid being left behind. He didn't want to help the nation or create jobs or change the world, he just wanted a position of power and was determined to get it. At any cost.

Harding's strategy of presenting a sweet front while cheating to get what he wants can be seen in everything he has ever done. It was widely believed, for example, that Harding's wife, Florence, ran the house while the timid, doting Harding trailed behind with his head lowered and his tail between his legs, yet nothing could be further from the truth. In 1905, Harding seemed to be Florence's obedient puppy dog, but all the while he was having a secret relationship with a young Ohio woman named Carrie Phillips.

While plenty of presidents have had affairs, Harding's is one of the sneakiest and sleaziest. Harding began his affair in the spring of 1905, while his wife was in Columbus undergoing treatment for a kidney ailment, and Carrie's husband,

James—Harding's longtime friend—had checked himself into the Battle Creek Sanitarium, a health resort in Michigan. It has absolutely nothing to do with his presidency, but having an affair with his good friend's wife while he's in a mental institution and *his own* wife is in a hospital reveals Harding's terrible character.

Right before the Republican Party decided to nominate Harding for the presidency, they asked him to search his soul and come clean with any skeletons in his closet. He spent ten minutes searching his conscience before calmly and confidently saying, *"Nope. Nothing."* Minutes later, he was nominated. In 1921, we made him the twenty-ninth president of the United States. Years after his first affair, but not before his last, including one with someone thirty years his junior.

Notice the patterns? Harding wants you to think he's a nice gentleman, but he'll crush your newspaper and destroy your reputation if you stand in his way. He'll appear to be the faithful, doting husband, but he'll cheat the second his wife has her back turned (or is receiving medical treatment).

Historians like to point out that Harding as a president wasn't corrupt—he just had the misfortune of having terrible friends—but make no mistake, there is a *reason* all those awful people gravitated toward Harding to begin with. Evil attracts more evil.

One of Harding's smartest career moves was quietly dying in office while traveling around the country in 1923. He had an enlarged heart, but not the kind the Grinch had—the kind that kills presidents. Mysterious circumstances surrounded his death, but no autopsy was done, presumably because the coroners figured that if he was poisoned, he was sort of asking for it.

OFFICIAL FANTASY DREAM TEAM RATING

Boooo. Noooooo! Harding stinks.

30

CALVIN COOLIDGE
THE SILENT KILLER

Presidential Term: 1923–1929
Political Party: Republican
Spouse: Grace Goodhue
Children: John and Calvin Jr.
Birthdate: July 4, 1872
Death Date: January 5, 1933
Fun Fact: Coolidge was the last president
not to have a personal telephone.

There's no real way to sugarcoat this: John Calvin Coolidge's biography reads like the chilling origin story of a serial killer. Even the nickname Silent Cal, assigned to the man because he was famously shy and quiet, calls to mind visions of some creepy, looming bedside murderer. But Silent Cal grew up to be the thirtieth president of the United States, and *not* some kind of eerily quiet murderer who stalked campgrounds.

Probably.

Like a lot of kids, Coolidge was told at an early age that he was not allowed to make mistakes. Unlike a lot of kids, he was often reminded by his parents that he was never going to be the smartest or strongest in his class, so he had better work harder than anyone to be the *best*. Coolidge followed his parents' orders, worked harder than anyone, and ended up really excelling in school. Is this because he was a good kid who wanted nothing more than to please his folks? No. It's because on the rare occasions when he did make a mistake (say, by being late for school), he would be banished to a cold attic, empty but for cobwebs, where he would be forced to sit in the dark and wait. For *hours.*

His father, while stern and terrifying, was often away on business, so Coolidge was primarily raised by his grandmother (also stern and terrifying—she was the one who locked him in the attic). People called Coolidge Silent Cal because he rarely spoke, but few realize that even into his presidency, he spoke at length to his mother. Or, rather, his *dead* mother, who died when he was twelve. He revealed this in letters to his father, who never responded to the admission. (Coolidge's dead mother also refused to comment.)

Even though he lost his mother and should have been allowed some time to grieve, Coolidge had to continue his quest to be the best. He just stayed focused and kept working hard. Several years later, his fifteen-year-old sister, Abbie, died. Despite that loss, and even though he regularly wrote letters to his father talking about how miserable and lonely he was (also unanswered), Coolidge kept on keeping on. He went on to excel in college, law school, and as governor of Massachusetts, because make no mistake, he would make no mistakes. He was conditioned to believe a terrifying attic was lurking behind every mistake, and he was *not* going back there. So all that stress, all that grief, and all that tension was kept locked up inside.

After the corruption-filled nightmare of the Harding administration, it was up to Coolidge to assure the American people that order and integrity had been restored to the White House. He needed to convince everyone that a coolheaded and honest man was running the country, and he did.

For a little while.

Then a few years into his presidency, Coolidge had to watch his sixteen-year-old son, Calvin Jr., die in a freak tennis accident. (He stubbed his toe playing tennis, the toe got infected, and the infection killed him.) This was, we can say, the final tragic straw that broke Coolidge's back. Tragedy and death followed him everywhere, but unlike Andrew Jackson, who ate and subsequently drew tremendous strength from death, Coolidge dwelled on it with the morbid obsession of Jack the Ripper. He had the Secret Service regularly bring young boys around the White House to say hi to the president, just so he could still feel connected to his son in some way. (He requested no other guests, just wave after wave of surrogate Calvin Juniors.) He could only talk, think, and write about his departed son, often mentioning the passing of his son to every White House guest, *as if they somehow hadn't heard.*

Calvin Jr.'s death destroyed Coolidge and his presidency. When Junior was alive, Coolidge was the dynamic and progressive president who made demands of Congress and proudly boasted to his father that "men do what I tell them to do." After

Junior died, he was the president who rarely spoke to Congress (or anyone else); got almost nothing done; and stayed inside all day, sleeping through his depression.

Or, not *just* napping. Occasionally he would take some time to be emotionally distant to his wife and flip out on his staff. This was a man, remember, who was surrounded by tragedy but kept all his frustrations and heartbreak locked up inside, because he never wanted to let down his stern, distant father by showing that he was anything less than perfect. No one can keep that kind of rage at bay forever; Coolidge was a time bomb, *tick, tick,* ticking away.

Coolidge kept the White House staff, according to some employees, "in a state of constant anxiety" with his "volcanic eruptions of temper." One White House employee said that "[t]hose who saw Coolidge in a rage were simply startled," and that Teddy Roosevelt "in his worst temper . . . was calm compared with Coolidge." Teddy

Roosevelt got his face on Mount Rushmore simply by head butting the mountain (probably), and Coolidge at his craziest made Teddy look like a *pussycat*.

Still, Coolidge's story isn't *just* about horrible tragedy and premature death. He's also just really weird, in a general sort of way, and might have been part Tarzan. He had a pet hippo that he often visited at the National Zoo in Washington, D.C., and he was frequently seen walking around the White House followed by wild animals, including a pet raccoon, which would cling to his neck.

Depressed, tired, and broken, Coolidge decided not to seek reelection after his first term, which caught even his wife by surprise, as he had not mentioned it to her before announcing it publicly. (Man, he really *was* silent.)

OFFICIAL FANTASY DREAM TEAM RATING

Maybe he could be your **Loose Cannon,** because he was so crazy and quick to anger. But I don't want to say that if it'll bother Coolidge. I'm too afraid to say the wrong thing, so just use your best judgment. This is on you.

31

HERBERT HOOVER

IS THE RAMBO OF PRESIDENTS

Presidential Term: 1929–1933
Political Party: Republican
Spouse: Lou Henry
Children: Herbert Jr. and Allan
Birthdate: August 10, 1874
Death Date: October 20, 1964
Fun Fact: Hoover was the first man to be president without serving in a war or holding previous public office.

If you were looking for a good reason to fear thirty-first president Herbert Hoover, you came to the right place (for this information, and absolutely nothing else). Hoover isn't afraid to die, because he already died once before and decided that it wasn't so bad. When Hoover was two, his parents thought he was dead. They found him unresponsive and motionless after suffering through a nasty bout of croup (an infection causing bad coughs and shortness of breath), so they put pennies over his eyes, covered him up with a sheet (which was the custom at the time when people died), and then pronounced him dead (which is *still* the custom when people die).

He survived, obviously, and he held on to those survival skills. When his father died four years later, Hoover carried on, and when his mother died less than four years after that, leaving Hoover an orphan at nine years old, he just kept surviving. With no parents to either raise or protect him, Hoover lived with his grandmother for a while, but he mostly spent time with a gang of young Native American boys who taught him how to hunt, use a bow and arrow, and generally survive anywhere in the wild. Two years later, he was sent to live with an uncle in Oregon who raised the young Hoover using slightly edited passages from the Bible. "Turn your cheek once," Hoover's uncle instructed, "but if he smites you again, then punch him." (For any readers who aren't Bible scholars who are wondering which part wasn't in the Bible, it was the "punch your enemies" part.)

So what happens to a boy whose parents first leave him for dead and then just straight up leave him? He grows up to be the most self-reliant president we've ever had. He was focused, efficient, and fearless, and he expected the same from everyone he encountered; if they *didn't* meet his expectations, he'd leave them behind.

Hoover lived by a simple motto: "Work is life." Hoover never sought power; he just liked to work hard and do good in the world. After earning his way through college through various odd jobs, he landed a job with a gold-mining company, which led to great fortune. Once he'd turned some money into lots of money and then lots of money into a TON of money, Hoover turned his focus to humanitarian efforts, distributing food and supplies to American troops during World War I.

Having received national attention for these humanitarian efforts, Hoover was asked to meet with the German enemy commanders in the middle of the war and negotiate to bring aid to the American prisoners of war. As people who managed but didn't actually fight wars, Hoover, his team, and the German commanders met in a comfortable room and sipped martini after martini while discussing, you know, all those human lives.

But Hoover was secretly working the room for his country. He gave his team and the bartender strict orders; no matter what the Germans did, the Americans were going to keep their wits about them. He told the bartender to pour only *water* in the American martinis, and save all the gin for the Germans. But Hoover couldn't just trust the bartender to know which drink was which; he needed a way to tell his drinks from the Germans', so he demanded that all the American drinks be served with an onion garnish (instead of the traditional olive). To avoid suspicion, he assured the Germans that this was simply how Americans took their martinis (though the truth was that he just wanted to make sure no German accidentally grabbed the wrong drink, exposing his trickery).

The plan worked. The Americans kept their heads on straight and negotiated brilliantly, while the Germans got drunker and sloppier, giving the American negotiators the advantage. Hoover got what he wanted: he convinced the Germans to let him behind enemy lines to deliver food to the starving civilians. And as a bonus, the drink that Hoover threw together on the spot to fool the Germans actually caught on in America. The Gibson martini (named after the general who accompanied Hoover) is still popular even today. Talk about efficiency. Hoover was so efficient that even with lives on the line, he thought, *I know I'm only doing this to help my scheme, but I might as well make a dynamite drink and immortalize my friend in the process. Ole Two Birds Hoover, that's what they'll call me.*

(No one ever would.)

Hoover continued his humanitarian work, even making sure to give aid to starving Europeans after the war, and when Calvin Coolidge announced that he wouldn't run for office in the 1928 election, Hoover threw his hat in the ring. It wasn't that he grew up dreaming to be president; it just seemed like a job that would allow him to do the greatest amount of good for the greatest amount of people. Hoover's stellar reputation ensured an easy, landslide victory. Pretty good win for a guy who died at two.

Hoover wasn't our greatest president, but he was certainly one of our most driven. He rarely took vacations as president, and any time he wasn't working, he was antsy and uncomfortable, distracted by the amount of work that he could and should be getting done. He avoided trips and most hobbies, and it was said that he would eat his entire four-course dinner in eight minutes. It's normal for a president to skip a vacation here or there, but Hoover trained himself to wolf down food as efficiently as possible just so he had more time to *work*.

Hoover did enjoy *some* diversions. Every morning except Sunday, Hoover would wake up and play a spirited game of "Hooverball." Hooverball is similar to volleyball, except instead of hitting a soft, bouncy volleyball back and forth, players stand on opposite sides of a tall net throwing and catching a ten-pound medicine ball. A close friend of the president described it as "more strenuous than either boxing, wrestling, or football," and Hoover played it six days a week.

Despite how beloved and effective he was before his presidency, nothing was going to help Hoover once he took office. Almost immediately after he stepped into

Washington
Hoovers
World Champs of
Hooverball 1930

the White House, the stock market crashed and he made wrong decision after wrong decision, leading us into the Great Depression. Hoover was, remember, the self-reliant president. As a result, he would always strive to *reduce* the amount of government intervention in people's lives. He believed that the road to a better America starts at home, with everyone doing their part on their own. This is a great sentiment, and it might even work in some circumstances, but not during the greatest economic recession so far in America's history. Hoover, who stepped into the office vowing to end poverty in America, oversaw the beginning of a decade of increasing poverty with high unemployment and low profits.

Is Hoover *responsible* for the stock market crash or the Great Depression that followed? Of course not. These things happen as a result of various financial conditions, better explained by an economist and not some idiot who likes presidents (me, the person who wrote the book you're reading). But Hoover certainly didn't help things. Remember, when he saw America going to war, he *himself* decided to send money and food to the American soldiers. And when the war ended, it was again *his personal decision* to help the struggling Europeans. He believed that when the chips were down in America, privately owned relief organizations—NOT the government—should and *would* step in to save the country, out of the goodness of their hearts, the way he had done years earlier. Well, not everyone is as nice as Hoover, and his faith in private relief organizations was, sadly, misplaced. No one ever stepped up. The banks kept failing, and one in four Americans were put out of work.

Hoover lost reelection to Franklin Roosevelt in a landslide, and even though he spent the rest of his life committed to public service, nothing would ever change the association of the name Hoover with the Depression and suffering. To many Americans, he was the man who did nothing to help them while they lost their jobs and homes and struggled to feed their families.

OFFICIAL FANTASY DREAM TEAM RATING

He was a good man and a definite survivor, but he's not quite *enough* to warrant any spot on your Fantasy Dream Team (though maybe he could provide the refreshments).

THE PRESIDENTIAL ★ SCORECARD

Brains
Brawn
Loose Cannon
Moral Compass
Roosevelt...

32

FRANKLIN DELANO ROOSEVELT

ROLLING THUNDER

Presidential Term: 1933–1945

Political Party: Democratic

Spouse: Eleanor Roosevelt

Children: Anna, James, Franklin, Elliot, Franklin Delano Jr., and John

Birthdate: January 30, 1882

Death Date: April 12, 1945

Fun Fact: Roosevelt was one of four
U.S. presidents who used to be a cheerleader!

Franklin Delano Roosevelt's charisma, optimism, and foresight got us out of the Depression. His leadership skills set us up for victory in World War II, even though he wasn't around to see the final surrender. His effectiveness as a president got him elected for an unprecedented third and fourth term. He swam *several miles daily* despite his paralysis.

The Roosevelts are Just. The. Best.

FDR, one of our top two most Rooseveltian presidents (so far), was, like his fifth cousin TR, incredibly sick and close to death as a child. His mother was so worried that she kept him out of school and had him educated at home until he was fourteen. She also made him wear a dress for the first five years of his life, which doesn't inform FDR's presidency or personality, but I just think you should know about it. FDR used to wear dresses as a kid. People can be whatever they want to be and dress however they want. It's totally cool.

Whether he was wearing a dress or pants, FDR constantly suffered from headaches, harsh colds, influenza, pneumonia, chronic sinus trouble, occasional temporary paralysis, polio, and whatever else was around. If there was a bad disease in the early 1900s, FDR probably caught it and a number of other very serious things that should have killed him.

Unfortunately for disease, no one told FDR that he was supposed to die, so he never let any of his illnesses stop him. Whenever he wasn't bedridden, FDR could be found working out, swimming or boxing, making sure his precious windows of good health were spent on physical improvement. Everything was looking great, but then that pesky polio showed up. One day in 1921, Roosevelt went sailing and fishing, helped some locals put out a forest fire on his way home, went for a swim, and then jogged a mile. Two days later he couldn't move his legs, and the doctors diagnosed it as polio. They told him he wouldn't be able to walk again, and his mother and friends said it was time to retire and take life easy (though his wife, Eleanor, always pushed him to get back into politics, knowing he wouldn't be happy without it).

For anyone else, that would be the end of the story, but we're not dealing with anyone else here. The biggest mistake anyone can ever make is telling Franklin Delano Roosevelt that he can't do something. Through years of rigorous and painful exercise, FDR massaged and worked his leg muscles enough that, with the help of iron braces and canes, he was able to stand and walk again. As far as retirement and "taking life easy" went, FDR decided to become a state senator, then assistant secretary of the navy, and then governor of New York, and eventually settled into a relaxing career as president for longer than anyone else has ever been president.

No one really expected FDR to be president. People who saw him walking, only for short distances and always clutching a cane in one hand and the arm of either his son or an aide in the other, thought he was foolish to have any political hopes. Another Democrat, New York Governor Al Smith, asked FDR to introduce him at the 1924 Democratic National Convention. Al Smith wanted to run for president one day and thought a good word from FDR, a well-liked and respected man with a very influential last name, would do wonders for his political career. Friends of Smith asked him if he thought it was wise to give attention and a stage to someone who could turn out to be a political rival, but Smith wasn't worried because he assumed that Roosevelt would be dead within a year. FDR's speech was electrifying, and not long after that, *Roosevelt* was the governor of New York and eventually president, and Al Smith is some guy you've probably never heard of until right now.

FDR's struggle with illness and subsequent metal-wrapped life is remarkably similar to the story of another great leader who was part robot: Iron Man. FDR, much like Tony Stark, was cocky and arrogant before his life-changing diagnosis, but the years of suffering changed all that, and he emerged more humble, more fearless, and ready to defend America and the underdog. Also, FDR wore iron braces and used a wheelchair, which, for the purposes of this comparison, is *exactly* like a well-armed robot suit.

Scientifically speaking, being more presidential than other presidents was in FDR's blood. In addition to Teddy, FDR was related to Ulysses S. Grant, Zachary Taylor, and English prime minister Winston Churchill. You can't deny that the collection of ridiculously powerful DNA flowing through FDR's veins made it impossible for him NOT to be a great leader.

FDR won the presidency when America was in the worst shape it had been in since the Civil War. Twenty-five percent of American workers were jobless, two million people were homeless, and 40 percent of all banks were bankrupt. You'd have to be crazy to want to take over the country under those conditions, but Roosevelt was part RoboCop and *all* crazy. He was used to facing uphill battles, so he took the job and went to work immediately, passing a massive amount of new laws during his first hundred days in office. FDR's New Deal (his laws and executive orders designed to get the economy going again and to provide relief and create government jobs until things improved) assured the American people that he was rescuing the United States from the Great Depression, and at the time, it certainly seemed like it was. He presented himself as the opposite of Hoover (even though FDR was ALSO a millionaire). Americans saw Hoover, Roosevelt's predecessor, as a do-nothing millionaire who sat around while the country fell apart. Roosevelt, on the other hand, declared in his inaugural address that "this nation asks for action, and action now," and he was prepared to give it to them. FDR and his New Deal were here to save us.

The truth, which we now know thanks to being in the future, is that the New Deal *didn't* end the Great Depression, technically. In fact, four million *more* people lost their jobs during the beginning of FDR's presidency. His many new agencies and programs put people to work on the government's dime, but permanent jobs from private employers were still scarce. Really, America's entrance into World War II is likely what saved the nation; the increase in jobs and government spending made necessary by the war put Americans back to work.

Still, we only know these facts *now*, because we live in the present (or the future, if you're reading this book many years after I'm dead, in what I hope will be the year 3000 or so). At the time, while we can admit that FDR didn't *technically* end the Depression, his policies helped people cope with the difficult times, and he radiated a confidence that made the country *believe* things were better.

Convincing people of the impossible or unusual was FDR's bag. During the entirety of his extra-long run as president, he convinced the press not to take pictures of him in a wheelchair or discuss that he used one and needed to be lifted into beds at night. Whenever he was in public, he would walk with braces and a cane and a little help from his friends, but at all other times he was confined to a wheelchair—and because of the press's cooperation, the American people didn't know about it until 1945. Nowadays, the press demands to be told what the president ate for breakfast or what he named his dog or where he's going on vacation. People have clamored about wanting to see sitting president Barack Obama's extended birth certificate on the grounds that they have the right to know that information. In the 1930s, the president of the United States was in a wheelchair and *the American public didn't know about it.*

Anyway, back to the New Deal. FDR's New Deal didn't completely fix the economy, but because he *said* it did, he pumped Americans full of faith and hope. Roosevelt's will was more powerful than reality. He steered us through World War II and was elected to an unprecedented fourth term. He also established Social Security, a safety net we still rely on today. He needed to die in office—it was the only way Americans would stop voting for him. I *still* write him in on the ballot every four years.

OFFICIAL FANTASY DREAM TEAM RATING

FDR was described by President Lyndon Johnson as "the one person I ever knew, anywhere, who was never afraid." After overcoming the illness that resulted in his paralysis, FDR reportedly said, "If you ever spent two years in bed trying to wiggle your big toe, after that everything else would seem easy." I'm going to say what I've only been able to say once before: He is a great candidate for your **Roosevelt.**

★ 33 ★

IF YOU CAN'T TAKE

HARRY S. TRUMAN'S

HEAT, GET OUT OF HIS KITCHEN

Presidential Term: 1945–1953
Political Party: Democratic
Spouse: Bess Wallace
Children: Margaret
Birthdate: May 8, 1884
Death Date: December 26, 1972
Fun Fact: Truman played piano for two hours every single morning.

Many of our presidents have had tough, or at least inspiring, early lives. Lincoln was born in a log cabin and rose up to become president. Hoover cheated death. Grant was born in a barrel of whiskey and raised by snakes (probably).

Harry S. Truman—not so much.

Unlike Andrew Jackson, who looked for fights as a child with the manic eagerness of someone who believed candy would fly out if he beat his enemies like a piñata, Truman ran from fights. Literally. Schoolyard bullies often chose Truman as their target, and he chose the "flight" option and bolted at the first sign of trouble. Truman preferred to spend his childhood reading or braiding his sister's hair. His only childhood injury of note was a broken collarbone, which he received when he accidentally knocked himself out of his chair *while combing his hair,* which is the most embarrassing way to break your collarbone that doesn't involve pooping yourself.

For a long time, Truman was very unremarkable. He spent many years trying to start businesses so that he could have enough money to leave home (he lived on a farm that was *also* very unremarkable), but he failed consistently. Business after business went under, sending Truman deeper and deeper into debt. For the first twenty years of his life or so, it seemed Truman was as good at running a business as he was at not breaking his collarbone after brushing his precious hair too hard (which is to say, not very).

But it looks like Truman got all the cowardice and failure out of his system early, because all that fight fleeing and hair braiding stopped dead when he grew up. Somehow decades of running from fights turned into a burning desire to get into fights when he was older, which might be why he signed up to fight in World War I back in 1917. Despite how bad he was at literally everything he'd ever tried, Truman advanced quickly in the military and, in 1918, was made captain of Battery D (also known as Dizzy D), a unit of 194 soldiers who were known for their drunkenness and rowdiness. This was a unit that many considered uncommandable, and in fact Truman was made captain of their regiment only because they'd already driven the previous two captains away with their wild antics and refusal to listen to authority. Most assumed that Truman, with his limited fighting experience and his nerdy glasses, would quit.

But he surprised everyone when he turned the uncommandable unit of drunken jerks into a well-disciplined and efficient fight squad in just a few weeks. Truman spoke to them plainly, simply, and in a language they understood (which, in Battery D's case, meant a ton of cursing). Truman warned his troops that if any of them didn't think they could get along with him, he would punch them in the nose (because that would make them get along with him better?). On the subject of cursing, one of his soldiers said, "I never heard a man cuss so well or so intelligently . . . The battery didn't say a word. They must have figured the cap'n could do the cussin' for the whole outfit."

Just one month after Truman took command, the unit came under fire from their German enemies, and when the men panicked and tried to flee (running, as Truman so often had as a child, from the fight), Truman stood his ground and started yelling and cursing at the men. He screamed and insulted and belittled

anyone who tried to leave, letting run a string of profanities. The men of Battery D were so moved by Truman's determination and filthy mouth that, one by one, they all came back and stood with their captain, all while still under enemy fire. This band of unruly jerks was prepared to stay and die for Truman! Lucky for them, they never actually needed to; Truman marched his unit all over France, taking out Germans every step of the way, and never lost a single man. Maybe if one of the German soldiers had handed Truman a comb, things would have been different, but instead, Truman left the war a hero.

After the war, Truman *again* tried to start a business, this time a haberdashery (a fancy term for "a place that sells hats and men's clothing"), but that business *also* failed. The writing on the wall was clear: Truman had no place in the business world because he needed to LEAD. After abandoning the failed haberdashery business, he then turned his war hero status into a job in politics. As a Missouri senator, Truman became well known for his decency and honesty. He was a hard worker who spent his time cracking down on corruption in the government—the military in particular. He formed special committees that were put in place to make sure that no money was being wasted and that none of the weapons, vehicles, and uniforms America's soldiers were using were defective or shoddy.

He did *such* a good job that President Roosevelt demanded that Truman be his vice president leading into his final term. At first it was just a request, but when Truman seemed reluctant to take the job, it *became* a demand. As tough and confident as he had become in the war, Truman was still nervous at heart. When he'd learned that FDR had handpicked him as his vice president, Truman freaked out. And when he took the oath of office after FDR died, he told the press, "Boys, if you ever pray, pray for me now. I don't know if you fellas ever had a load of hay fall on you, but when they told me what happened yesterday, I felt like the moon, the stars, and all the planets had fallen on me."

When FDR died, he thrust Truman into the presidential . . . throne? Hammock? I don't know where presidents sit. Beanbag chair, probably . . . Anyway, Truman stepped up. Filling in for one of the greatest presidents we've ever had was no easy feat. FDR was a tough act to follow, but just as he surprised everyone during the war, Truman went on to become one of our most respected leaders.

Still, like most presidents, Truman had a sneaky, devious side too. He brought his honesty and integrity into the White House, but he didn't hold on to it for long; he made tough choices when he felt like he needed to. Tough and—let's say—unpresidential and possibly illegal choices.

Put yourself in Truman's shoes: It's 1947 and World War II is over, but you still want to keep a large military presence in Eastern Europe to keep the Soviets from taking over governments in other European countries like Hungary and Austria. Unfortunately, the American people don't *want* to devote the time, money, and resources that such a thing would require, because Americans in 1947 didn't really give a hoot about what happened to the government in Austria. But you're not the American people; you're President Truman. And you *want* that strong, powerful international presence. You want to go over to Europe and establish America as an international peacemaker/police force. So what do you do? You convince the country that they're a heartbeat away from another war.

You lie.

It's true that the Soviets in the 1940s weren't exactly the good guys, but that doesn't change the fact that Truman manipulated information and had people outright lie for him to scare the American people. Truman had Lucius Clay, the commander of military forces in Germany (and a man who personally believed that American troops in Eastern Europe were "as secure . . . as they would be at home"), write a letter to Congress claiming he believed that war could break out at any minute. He ordered a *general* who wrote private letters talking about how secure everyone was to *lie to Congress* to scare the American people enough to get approval for whatever Truman wanted for this alleged looming war.

The truth was that the Soviet Union was in no real shape to wage a war at the time; they simply weren't strong enough. But Truman wanted the draft reinstated and more money for the military, so he bent and broke the truth and warned everybody about a war that wasn't coming. (It worked, by the way.)

Truman may have made a name for himself in politics by seeking and taking out corruption in government committees, but he is one sneaky guy. He's not one of the bigger or stronger presidents, but he's certainly one of the most devious, especially when he thinks he's right. Like Jackson, Truman had a fiery temper and wasn't afraid to show it off, so much so that David Lilienthal, chairman of the Atomic Energy Commission, was genuinely afraid that Truman's tendency to occasionally flip out would bring about World War III. That's not hyperbole. Truman was the only president who actually dropped the atomic bomb—twice. *This was a real concern.*

Oh, speaking of the bomb, we should probably cover that, because the atomic bomb was a new and devastating piece of technology, and using it became the defining moment of Truman's presidency. Shortly after he took office, he was told that America had secretly developed an atomic bomb. He wrote in his diary that "we have discovered the most terrible bomb in the history of the world." Dropping two atomic bombs on Japan, killing over 125,000 people including civilians, was always going to be a controversial decision, but Truman believed for the rest of his life that it was the right one. He maintained that using the bomb saved lives and money in the long run. He knew he had a bomb that would *absolutely* end this war—how could he justify *not* using it? Without the bomb, American ground troops would have had to invade Japan for a very costly land war that could have lasted for who *knows* how long and killed countless American and Japanese soldiers and Japanese civilians. Instead, Harry Truman ordered the bombing of Hiroshima, and after Japan still didn't surrender, he ordered the bombing of Nagasaki. A few days after that second bomb was dropped, Japan surrendered unconditionally.

OFFICIAL FANTASY DREAM TEAM RATING

Truman's deviousness makes him a pretty good fit for your **Brains.** He knew how to look at a battlefield and the country like a chessboard—he could see ahead into what a situation would *eventually* need, and he knew how to move the pieces around to achieve whatever he wanted.

DWIGHT D. EISENHOWER

LIKE "IKE" OR HE'LL STRIKE YOU!

Presidential Term: 1953–1961

Political Party: Republican

Spouse: Mamie Doud

Children: Doud and John

Birthdate: October 14, 1890

Death Date: March 28, 1969

Fun Fact: In 1948, BOTH major political parties tried to get
Eisenhower to run for president under their banner.
He decided to remain in the military.

While we know now that most presidents were super crazy, there's a fairly clear pattern to the *kind* of craziness. Modern presidents were crazy *ambitious* and obsessed with power to an unhealthy degree, while early presidents were crazy in a more general, certifiable sort of way. A way that develops when you're born before laws have been invented.

Dwight D. Eisenhower ("Ike"), our thirty-fourth president, bucked the trend of modern presidents and embraced a tradition of old-school aggressive insanity pioneered by men like Andrew Jackson and George Washington. He was an early 1800s kind of crazy in a 1960s world. Even his name was tough: "Eisenhower" is German for "one who cuts iron," meaning Ike was born several degrees more awesome than you, right at birth.

Ike spent most of his childhood getting into fistfights and settling real or imagined scores with enemies using his tiny, bare fists. If he didn't have any schoolyard bullies to take on, Eisenhower would take on nature—when he wasn't allowed out on Halloween once as a child, he punched a tree trunk until his knuckles bled. Rumor has it that if you listen closely every October 31, you can still hear that tree crying, desperately trying to figure out what it had to do with Ike's Halloween.

When Ike grew up and ran out of trees to humiliate, he served in the army and excelled at it. Ike's military career spans over forty years of service, beginning in 1917. While a football injury prevented Ike from ever actually being a *part* of military action, he thrived as a commander, a man who had a high military IQ and knew how to plan attacks and inspire men to follow him. Ike was so good in the military that he never really tried to do anything else. In between World War I and World War II, Eisenhower still stuck around in the general field of warfare, even though there were no wars to fight. He studied military history and worked on and wrote about tanks. It's very likely, in fact, that Ike's decision to build up an Interstate Highway System as president was inspired by his time working on tanks. He didn't think the tanks were traveling across the country fast enough for his tastes, so he *built an entire highway system to speed things up.* He earned so many different military titles, some of which (military governor, supreme allied commander) sounded completely made up, and he even taught himself to fly a plane (even though no one asked him to), just in case he ever wanted to dabble in being a fighter pilot at some point. Ike was just a professional soldier, running tanks and protecting the country for his day job.

As Captain Doctor Supreme Allied Commander Wizard of Military Forces during World War II, Eisenhower orchestrated the 1944 Allied invasion of Normandy, made famous by the film *Saving Private Ryan* and one of the better Medal of Honor video games. Eisenhower originally scheduled the invasion for June 5, because the tides favored the Allies (there were only ten days in any given month when the tides *would* be favorable to an invasion of this kind), but he had to delay it due to bad weather that would have resulted in the loss of who *knows* how many troops. The weather was *also* supposed to be terrible on June 6, but Ike was tired of letting God delay his plans, so he risked everything and started the invasion. Even though a huge storm was *supposed* to hit and ruin all of Ike's plans, it didn't, and the weather cleared up at the last minute. Was it simply luck, or did nature retreat out of fear of Ike's wrath? It is the perhaps obvious stance of this book that luck had nothing to do with it; God had seen what Ike was capable of and would not dare cross him.

The invasion of Normandy was a major turning point in the war, and it allowed Ike to add "Superawesome Supreme Defeater of Adolf Hitler" to his already-impressive military résumé. When the war did end, Ike stuck around in Germany for a while, making sure civilians and former soldiers received food and aid before he returned to Washington to advise Truman as chief of staff of the army, yet another impossibly cool title.

When America ran out of made-up military titles to give Ike, they made him president. One of Ike's first orders of business involved looking to end the Korean War, a complex struggle that started as a civil war but went global, thanks to the Cold War fight between the Soviet Union and the United States, who were former allies. Seeing all the years of fighting with little progress and many lives lost, Ike thought, *Yeah, that's enough of that,* and ended it in one fell swoop. As much as Ike loved war, and as skilled as he was as a military strategist, he was an even bigger fan of peace. Eisenhower ended the Korean War during his presidency, and he did so without involving America in any other wars, because he wanted peace and believed it could be achieved. When the Department of Defense demanded more money for more bombs, Ike turned them down, asking, "How many times do we have to destroy Russia?" When Senator Joseph McCarthy went on the wild communist witch hunt that divided America, Eisenhower worked behind the scenes to get McCarthy censured (the political version of *"Shhhhhhh, that's enough of that"*). Eisenhower did this privately, by the way, because, in his words, he "refused to get in a pissing contest with a skunk," because presidents talked cooler back then than they do today. America "never lost a soldier or a foot of ground" during Ike's administration. President Eisenhower controlled the arms race and kept the peace. Under President Eisenhower, America also experienced an unparalleled prosperity that gave rise to teen culture. This is when rock and roll in America was born, with young folks running around and partying and dancing to Elvis Presley music, and it happened under Ike's watch.

Still, don't let Ike's peacekeeping and party allowing and never personally

serving on the front lines in any battle fool you into thinking our tree-fightingest president wasn't tough. By the time Ike was halfway through his presidency, he had had a messed-up knee, malaria, tuberculosis, high blood pressure, spinal malformation, shingles, neuritis, one heart attack, one stroke, Crohn's disease, and bronchitis. That's all according to his official medical history, but if you'd asked Eisenhower or read his diary at the time, you'd see that *he* casually summed up the whole ordeal by saying he had "lots of troubles with my insides lately." That's it. Not *"Boy, it sure feels like death inside my body, all the time, oh my God it hurts."* Just "lots of troubles . . . *lately.*"

It took *six* heart attacks to eventually kill Ike, and it's still not clear if the heart attacks did it or if Eisenhower simply willed himself to death. On what would turn out to be his deathbed, his last words were "I want to go. God take me." The message was clear: wars, diseases, and heart attacks don't stop Eisenhower; *he* decides when he's good and ready to die, and then you'd better do as he says.

OFFICIAL FANTASY DREAM TEAM RATING

Ike knew strategy, so if you need **Brains,** you wouldn't be wrong choosing Eisenhower. He was a student of warfare and would be a huge asset in whatever global emergency necessitates a Presidential Fantasy Dream Team.

★ 35

JOHN F. KENNEDY

AMERICA'S DASHING QUARTERBACK

Presidential Term: 1961–1963
Political Party: Democratic
Spouse: Jacqueline Bouvier
Children: Arabella, Caroline, John Jr., and Patrick
Birthdate: May 29, 1917
Death Date: November 22, 1963
Fun Fact: Kennedy was the first Catholic president.

From 1961 until 1963, the United States of America was a high school football team, and John F. Kennedy was the dreamy quarterback we all respected and lusted after. Plenty of presidents have been as good as Kennedy, and many have been *better*, but he is the only president who made the American people, in unison, say, *"What a cool dude. I wanna party with that guy."*

Kennedy's father, Joseph, raised his sons with the "Kennedy standards," which referred not to helping people or leading a good life, but to *winning*. Kennedy boys were told not to "play [a sport] unless you can be captain" and that "second place is failure." In fact, the only times Kennedy got emotional, according to his sister Eunice, were "when he loses." A few decades later, little Jack finally proved himself to his father by becoming captain of America.

JFK was our most James Bond–ian president, and not just because all the women loved him—he also had a proven track record of toughness to boot. Kennedy had a back injury that disqualified him from serving in the army, but instead of just seizing the opportunity to avoid getting shot at by bad guys without looking like a coward, he used his influential father's connections to sneak his way into the navy. That's right. While most overprivileged kids use their rich daddies to get out of speeding tickets or get into good colleges, Kennedy begged *his* father for a favor that would result in people trying to *shoot and kill him,* because Kennedy was a breed of real-life action hero we simply stopped making.

In August 1943, Kennedy's boat (the *PT-109*) was ripped in two by the Japanese destroyer *Amagiri.* The boat was destroyed, the crew was disoriented, and flames were everywhere, but Kennedy, even on his worst day, could not be shaken. He addressed his crew and asked if they wanted to fight or surrender. "There's nothing in the book about a situation like this," Kennedy said. "What do you want to do? *I have nothing to lose.*" (Whoever made the Hollywood movie based on the attacks on Kennedy's boat and crew should be kicked out of the business for calling it *PT 109* instead of *Nothing to Lose.* Come on, Hollywood.)

Kennedy, despite that chronic back injury and a newly ruptured spinal disc, swam four hours to an island with his crew. If you're not impressed by that, you should know that he did it while towing an injured crewman by the life-jacket strap. And if you're not impressed by that, you should know that he did the towing with his *teeth.* And if you're not impressed by that, you should know that when they realized there was no food on the island, they swam to a *new* island, with Kennedy *again* towing an injured crewman with his teeth. And if you're not impressed by *that, what is wrong with you?!*

One of the most interesting things about Kennedy is how well he protected his image. Everyone thinks of Kennedy as a young, athletic, "cool guy president," but it was all a carefully constructed charade. Despite all the impressive things written about Kennedy in books, including and especially this one, and despite him being the youngest man elected to the presidency at the time, he was actually a much weaker man than most people knew. Kennedy acted the part of a healthy young man of power, partly because he never wanted to give in to any of his illnesses, and partly to make the American people believe he was an energetic leader they could trust to be strong during the dangerous days of the Cold War. He was plagued by various conditions (including Addison's disease, an adrenal disease that causes weakness and abdominal pain) and was born with the left side of his body smaller than the right, which is what caused all his back problems. Kennedy's back was so bad that he wore a metal back brace, and when he was out of view of the press,

he would often use crutches or even a wheelchair to get around. The truth is that Kennedy was sick and in pain his entire life; he just refused to accept it because he didn't want it to hold him back (and because "Kennedy boys don't cry" was another one of the infamous Kennedy standards). He presented an image of vitality, but make no mistake—Kennedy was always hurting.

Image was everything to Kennedy. During the sixties, America and the Soviet Union were fighting each other all over the globe. Then the Soviets launched *Sputnik,* the first satellite, into space, and the Cold War was launched into orbit. As part of the space race, the Soviet Union wanted to be the first to put astronauts on the moon. Kennedys, you'll recall, can't settle for second place, so Kennedy made a big spectacle out of pushing for Americans to land on the moon first. He *tried* asking to work *with* the Soviets, so they could pool their efforts and get to the moon first together, but the Soviets declined. So Kennedy made it a singular focus to make sure America hit the moon first. At first this goal seemed as expensive as it was ridiculous. Kennedy met with top-level NASA scientists to ask about America's chances, and they unanimously agreed that landing on the moon was not an internal priority and there were much better ways to spend time and money. Kennedy didn't care. Landing on the moon was flashier, so that's what he wanted. We didn't actually land on the moon during his lifetime, but there's no question that Kennedy's drive and ambition got us there.

Constantly sick and accident-prone as a child, Kennedy thrived on the idea that death was constantly around the corner waiting for him. He'd had so many surgeries and life-threatening illnesses, and was on what many believed to be his deathbed at least *three separate times* in his life, that he lived every day like it might be his last. His personal secretary said that he tried "to crowd as much living as possible into every single hour." *That's* why he told his *PT-109* crew he had "nothing to lose" and was prepared to go into battle even after his boat was torn right in half, and that's why he drove himself to become the youngest president ever elected. It's arguable that he accomplished as much as he did in his brief presidency because the specter of premature death loomed over his shoulder at every waking minute.

An early death eventually DID come for Kennedy, but from the bullet of assassin Lee Harvey Oswald instead of one of his many diseases or injuries (though the assassination has inspired numerous conspiracy theories over the past fifty years, and many people remain unconvinced that Oswald was the only assassin—but that could take its own book to explain). Kennedy was riding in a blue limousine through Dallas, Texas, with his wife and some other guests, waving to and smiling at the crowd that had gathered to see him. Mrs. Connally, the wife of Texas's governor, turned to Kennedy to say, "You can't say that Dallas isn't friendly to you today," right before he was shot and killed. He was forty-six years old.

It's impossible to know what Kennedy would have done had his life and presidency not been tragically cut short. He's remembered fondly and remains one of the most famous presidents. He averted a nuclear war in the Cuban missile crisis, made great progress with the space program started during Eisenhower's administration, negotiated agreements with the Soviets to reduce nuclear stockpiles, established the Peace Corps, and, on top of all that, filled Americans with *hope*. He was young. He was exciting. Marilyn Monroe liked him. His wife was cool. He set us on course for *the moon*. He made Americans think they could be and achieve anything.

OFFICIAL FANTASY DREAM TEAM RATING

You want JFK on your Fantasy Dream Team, but it's hard to find a perfect fit. There are certainly smarter and stronger presidents, and he's not wild enough to be your **Loose Cannon.** My suggestion is to bring him on as your **Moral Compass,** not necessarily because he was always honest in his personal life (he, in fact, had many affairs with other women during his marriage), but because he was a real leader when America needed one and stood firm for the public's good. Kennedy knew how to get people to like and follow him. If you're building a Fantasy Dream Team, you'll need someone who can do the same—a Captain America around whom your other Presidential Avengers can rally.

36

LYNDON B. JOHNSON

THE PUPPET MASTER

Presidential Term: 1963–1969

Political Party: Democratic

Spouse: Lady Bird Taylor

Children: Lynda and Luci

Birthdate: August 27, 1908

Death Date: January 22, 1973

Fun Fact: There's an audio recording of Johnson talking to his tailor on the phone and burping loudly. Seriously; look it up, it's hilarious.

Pull just about any president out of a hat and you'll hear the same story: *"I had no ambition to be the president of the United States, but God [or 'the people'] seemed to want me to be president; I humbly accept God's plan and I am hereby announcing my candidacy for the presidency."* Washington created the mold by being the farmer who reluctantly became a soldier who reluctantly became a commander who reluctantly became a politician, and every president since followed in his faux-humble footsteps.

Except Lyndon B. Johnson.

Johnson always wanted to be the president. Always. In *grade school* Johnson was telling his classmates that he was going to be the president one day, and as he grew up, he never stopped saying "I want to be the president." He just altered it to "I want to be *the best* president." It takes an impossibly giant ego to look at the office of the presidency, in all its enormities and with all its responsibilities, and think, *I could do that.* Johnson looked at his heroes, like FDR, and thought, *I could do that better.*

This was because LBJ is the only president who was acutely aware of how *cool* it was to be president. He knew it was an important job, and one to be taken seriously, and yada yada yada, but he also knew it was pretty awesome. Johnson was addressing some troops in Vietnam, and after his speech, right when he was about to make his exit in a military helicopter, a member of his staff allegedly asked which helicopter was his and he (again, allegedly) replied, "Son, *all* these helicopters are mine." It wasn't *just* the coolness that attracted Johnson to the presidency; it was mostly the power, and to Johnson, power was *everything.*

Everything Johnson did as president was about demonstrating this power. Whenever he wanted something from a senator or visiting diplomat, he would employ what came to be known as the Johnson Treatment. Utilizing his impressive six-foot-three-inch frame, Johnson would get in that person's face and *loom* right over him, looking down at him as a physical reminder that Johnson's literal and figurative status dwarfs his. He would badger and yell and spit and mock, all while being just a few inches away from someone's face. It was about intimidation; everyone was powerless against the Johnson Treatment.

If towering over someone wasn't demeaning enough, he'd also make people watch him poop. If you needed to go over important business with the president, he'd listen for a bit and, every once in a while, have you follow him into the bathroom and plead your case while he nonchalantly pooped. If there's a more efficient demonstration of power, I've certainly never heard it (unless, of course, the president ever thought to combine the Johnson Treatment with the ole "watch me poop" technique).

Still, there's more to Johnson than just the way he pooped. This chapter is called "Puppet Master" because Johnson knew how to take control. He took control of the presidency after the shocking death of JFK, and he took control of all his opponents. He kept a folder of information on every single person in the Senate. He knew what they wanted, what they liked, and what their weaknesses were. Biographer Doris Kearns Goodwin states that he would "get up every day and learn what their fears, their desires, their wishes, their wants were and he could then manipulate, dominate, persuade and cajole them." If he was dealing with a particularly short senator, he'd grab him by the lapels and lift him straight into the air. He was like a big presidential bully, cornering members of the Senate and leaning over them while they backpedaled helplessly, badgering them until they submitted to his demands. *"Stop hitting yourself,"* he probably said to one or two uppity senators, while whipping them with their own useless hands.

As president, Johnson was an idealist. He wanted America to be a "Great Society," where all the children are educated, all the lakes and oceans are clean, and everyone is kind and encouraging. After President Kennedy's assassination, Johnson served out the remainder of Kennedy's term, and then easily won the 1964 election against Barry Goldwater, winning by over sixteen million votes. (For context, Kennedy beat Nixon in 1960 by only a little over one hundred thousand votes.) In stark contrast with Kennedy's tragically shortened presidency, Johnson got to work and immediately started getting legislation passed, a skill he learned after spending years in the Senate. All this legislation went toward building Johnson's Great Society—reducing taxes to fight poverty, advancing civil rights, and providing health care for the poor

and elderly with Medicaid and Medicare. He established the National Endowment for the Arts, providing money for artists and creators, and worked diligently to preserve parks and keep the air clean. He passed the Civil Rights Act in 1964 (criminalizing discrimination in employment) and the Voting Rights Act in 1965 (putting a stop to any barrier aimed at keeping black people from voting). Johnson did more for black Americans than any president since Lincoln.

Then, unfortunately (for everyone), the Vietnam War broke out, and it fell to Johnson to decide what America's role would be. Johnson, a peace-loving man who wanted to spend his entire presidency making America great, immediately knew that he needed to intervene in Vietnam, and he *further* knew that, no matter what happened, America's involvement in Vietnam would define his presidency. He knew that the war would be a distraction from his Great Society and could be used as a tool by his opponents; as long as there was a war going on involving young American soldiers, it needed to take precedence over all of Johnson's other policies. He also knew that if he *didn't* intervene, America would look weak and our international opponents would attack. In his own words, "I knew from the start that I was bound to be crucified either way I moved."

We'll never see the full realization of Johnson's Great Society. The Vietnam War and the American protests that followed absolutely absorbed Johnson's presidency and legacy. Americans did not support the war and, as a result, didn't support Johnson. He did not seek reelection and went home to Texas.

OFFICIAL FANTASY DREAM TEAM RATING

That was *such a bummer* of an ending, but please don't forget what a cool guy Johnson was. He'd be a great fit for your **Brains,** or any job that requires strategic pooping.

★ 37 ★

RICHARD NIXON

DESERVES HIS BAD REPUTATION

Presidential Term: 1969–1974
Political Party: Republican
Spouse: Pat Ryan
Children: Tricia and Julie
Birthdate: January 9, 1913
Death Date: April 22, 1994
Fun Fact: Nixon is literally the only president
I don't want to hang out with.

Richard Nixon will forever go down in history as one of the worst presidents of all time, and that is a fact. History will never vindicate his actions. He'll be associated with sliminess and an inflated sense of jowly entitlement for the rest of human existence. His excessive sweatiness in the first televised debates are the reasons why every presidential campaign today has a budget for a wardrobe and makeup specialist.

His hideousness invented a job.

Before all that, Nixon was practically born to be horrible. He was sick his entire life and never well liked, and psychoanalysts and historians who have looked into Nixon's character have described him as "a man torn by inner conflict, lonely, hypersensitive, narcissistic, suspicious, and secretive" and a man who "lied to gain love, to shore up his grandiose fantasies, to bolster his ever-wavering sense of identity. He lied in attack, hoping to win."

Nixon had two nicknames his whole life: Gloomy Gus (given to him in college because of his constant seriousness) and Tricky Dick (which he earned because of his trickiness). He served in the navy but saw no actual combat, hated sports, never exercised, and was once called no good by Harry S. Truman. All the facts in this paragraph are unrelated; I just wanted to list a bunch of awful Nixon things.

One of the most unfortunate things about Nixon from a critical perspective is that he *did* do a few good things while in office. He extended America's reach all the way to the moon (really fulfilling *Kennedy's* promise), and even though we can't do anything with it or ever hang out there, it's important to know that it's ours and no one else is allowed to touch it. Nixon got us out of Vietnam (after a prolonged and humiliating defeat) and was the first American president to visit China. There. I promised the publisher I'd spend at least one hundred words saying vaguely nice things about Nixon, just to make sure the book doesn't come off as too biased, and now that I've done that, we can move on to our regularly scheduled programming.

Did you know that President Tricky Dick plotted to kill someone while in office? True story. It wasn't an enemy of America, it was just an enemy of *Nixon's*. Jack Anderson was a journalist who chased Nixon throughout his entire career. Anderson believed Nixon was corrupt and dedicated his life to exposing that corruption, and it drove Nixon *crazy* because Anderson was pesky and manipulative, and *totally right*. Several confidential tapes reveal Nixon and his attorney general obsessing over Anderson and figuring out if they were going to discredit him or kill him. Nixon and his team thought about murdering Anderson by either hiding poison in his medicine cabinet or smearing a lethal dose of LSD on his steering wheel.

If plotting to kill and discredit one person isn't devious enough for you, Nixon also had no problem ruining the whole world. Nixon's opponent in the 1968 election, Hubert Humphrey (Johnson's vice president), was pulling ahead in the polls because he single-handedly made great strides toward peace in Vietnam leading up to the election. He called for a bombing halt and Vietnam *agreed*. America and North Vietnam were just a few days away from total peace, and the American people were a few days away from electing their next president, but Nixon just wanted to win, so none of that mattered to him. The day before the election, Nixon sabotaged the peace talks by convincing America's allies in South Vietnam to back out, warning them that they were going to get sold out if they went ahead with this whole peace thing. Without the momentum of the peace talks behind Humphrey, he lost the election to Nixon, who publicly criticized Humphrey for his inability to deliver.

Just to make sure this lands, here it is again: Nixon extended the war in Vietnam by five years just so he could cheat Humphrey out of the White House and become president.

But, hey, maybe Nixon had a *better* strategy to end the war. Maybe he had his

own plans for how to end the war and wanted to implement them as president. Maybe it was even more peaceful, right?

Well, he did have his own strategy, but if you know your history, you already know that Nixon's plan *wasn't* more peaceful than Humphrey's. Nixon favored what he called the madman theory, but what is commonly known among pop culture enthusiasts like you and me as the good cop/bad cop routine. Nixon wanted to convince the North Vietnamese that he was *crazy* and could snap at any minute. Nixon legitimately said to his advisors, "We'll just slip them the word that, 'for God's sake, you know Nixon is obsessed about Communism. We can't constrain him when he's angry—and he has his hand on the nuclear button.'" Nixon *said that!* It would have been pretty cool, except the problem is that every bad cop needs a good cop, and Nixon didn't have one, because there's only one president. So there was no good cop being reasonable and calming down the bad cop; there was just the bad cop who admitted to wanting to bomb North Vietnam off the planet and *almost tried.* In 1972, he bombed for twelve straight days.

Eventually, Nixon did effectively end American involvement in the Vietnam War. Not thanks to the madman theory, obviously—that's idiotic—but because Nixon agreed to remove all troops and spend some time and money rebuilding North Vietnam, as long as American prisoners of war were returned. Call it "retreating," or "very expensive retreating," if you want to split hairs, but Nixon did get our troops home. He got them home from a war that *could* have ended already if he hadn't extended it five years for his own political gain, but he still got them home. Yay, Nixon.

After years of questionable ethics, Nixon was finally brought down by the Watergate scandal, when he directed his staff to cover up a bungled attempt to steal documents from the Democratic National Committee. Nixon was famously impeached by the House Judiciary Committee for obstruction of justice and abuse of power, and resigned the presidency—the only president in history to do so. Much to everyone's chagrin, Nixon was given a full pardon by his successor, Gerald Ford. He was never indicted for any of the horrible things he did, only a *fraction* of which are covered in this chapter, and he spent the rest of his life dismissing the crimes as simple "blunders."

OFFICIAL FANTASY DREAM TEAM RATING

Richard Nixon is one of the most dangerous men in this book. He does not belong on your Fantasy Dream Team; in fact, if a Presidential Fantasy Dream Team is ever required, it's probably because of something Nixon did.

THE PRESIDENTIAL ★ SCORECARD

? Brains
? Brawn
? Loose Cannon
? Moral Compass
? Roosevelt...

38

GERALD FORD

CAN'T STOP FALLING DOWN

Presidential Term: 1974–1977
Political Party: Republican
Spouse: Betty Bloomer
Children: Michael, John, Steven, and Susan
Birthdate: July 14, 1913
Death Date: December 26, 2006
Fun Fact: Ford's real first name was Leslie.

Gerald Ford will only be remembered for two things: his pardoning of Richard Nixon and his inexplicable tendency to fall down with shocking regularity. Few people know Ford was an athlete his whole life, excelling at football through high school and college. His coaches often marveled at how sharp and meticulous he was, saying that having Ford on a team was like having an extra coach on the field. Ford's high football IQ, attention to detail, athleticism, and shockingly high threshold for taking blows to the head were so impressive that he was offered a huge salary to play professional football by both the Detroit Lions and the Green Bay Packers, but he turned them down and decided to focus on law. He didn't have enough money for law school (his grades weren't great), but he got accepted to Yale with the condition that he promise to coach Yale's undergraduate boxing program (he accepted).

That's only really striking when you realize that Ford had never boxed in his entire life. Yale took Ford on face value alone, saying, *"Your grades aren't quite good enough for law school, but we'll let that slide because you look like a man who*

★ 237 ★

could train people in how to beat up other people," and Ford simply responded, *"Sounds about right."* Because he didn't make enough money as a boxing coach, Ford spent his summers working as a professional bear feeder, which is a title I would *pretend* to hold to impress women if it didn't sound so completely made up. But it's true. Ford was a park ranger/bear feeder at Yellowstone National Park, because someone needed to feed the bears and that fell into the category of tough-guy things Ford assumed he'd rule at. He also worked as a male model in his late twenties, making it to the cover of *Cosmopolitan* magazine in 1942, which has absolutely nothing to do with his presidency; I just thought I'd mention it. He's a fairly average guy with a bunch of random jobs under his belt who ended up spending a ton of time in the White House; basically, Gerald Ford's life story is like a less believable *Forrest Gump.*

After the attack on Pearl Harbor, Ford put his law degree on hold and hung up his boxing gloves, his bear-feeding nunchucks, and his male model underpants so he could pursue killing all the bad guys who hated America. He joined the navy and quickly rose from ensign to lieutenant commander. He was then made a naval fitness instructor (teaching big, tough navy men how to be bigger, tougher, navy-er men). This might have been enough action for your average guy, but Ford was raised in the school of hard knocks (Yale, I guess?) and he wanted *more,* so he requested a transfer to the USS *Monterey,* a light aircraft carrier that fought in almost every major battle in the South Pacific. As if that wasn't enough, massive typhoons attacked the *Monterey* and three American destroyers. The other three ships capsized and lost most of their crew, and Ford's ship almost tipped over and burst into flames. As the ship tipped twenty-five degrees to one side, Ford lost his footing on the deck, started sliding toward the ocean, and would have fallen right in if he hadn't caught hold of the rim of the deck *with his foot.* He readjusted, got himself to a safe place on the boat, and put out the fire, which is *literally impossible.*

Ford never went to hide below deck; he just stood up top in the storm, watching his ship sway and burn, thinking, *Weird. I am super not afraid of death, it turns out.* By the time he left the war, Ford had accumulated ten battle stars. A man who has enough battle stars to comfortably throw a few of them at you like ninja shurikens and still have a bunch left over to intimidate bears is *not* a man to be messed with.

After the war, Ford was bitten by the politics bug and made a name for himself (not Leslie—a different name) as a hardworking, honest politician of integrity. He never lied, never told a half-truth, never manipulated anyone, and never did anything he didn't think was right. His moral streak earned the admiration of Republicans and Democrats alike. His Homer Simpson–esque plainspoken nature mixed well with his Homer Simpson–esque appearance. And he faced an uphill battle when Nixon resigned and he took over the presidency, because he was the first president to serve without being elected either president *or* vice president. When Nixon ran, Spiro Agnew was his running mate; THAT'S the ticket the American people voted for. But then Agnew resigned after a financial scandal and Nixon picked Ford to replace him, and then NIXON resigned, leaving America with some guy they never even had the CHANCE to vote for as their leader. But when he succeeded Nixon and promised to restore integrity and honesty to the White House, America was ready to believe him.

And then he pardoned Nixon and America was like, *"You jerk! We trusted you!"*

If you don't know, when the president "pardons" someone, that person is basically getting a get-out-of-jail-free card. The president takes someone who has committed or has been accused of committing crimes and essentially says, *"No one is allowed to prosecute or jail this person anymore; this person is no longer a criminal by order of the president."* If you became president and one of your friends got a speeding ticket, you could sign some paperwork that says your friend doesn't have to pay that ticket, and then your friend would owe you BIG time. (Presidents rarely do this, though.)

The hard truth is that pardoning Nixon was the right thing to do. Sure, letting Nixon get away with everything he had done over a five-year period without the courts ever determining his guilt or innocence is kind of a bummer. But Ford saw a country with a failing economy and a military that was second best in a time when second best wasn't an option, and all anyone wanted to talk about was "Nixon this and Nixon that." So Ford made the tough call and granted Nixon an absolute pardon, because it was a more official way of ending the conversation than saying, *"Just shut up and let me be president already."*

It was a tough call that wasn't going to earn Ford any friends (except Nixon, which, *gross*), but making tough calls was Ford all over. Unfortunately, Ford's decision to pardon Nixon unconditionally without even hearing what his crimes were ruined the reputation of honesty and openness he'd spent his life building (and would eventually be the singular issue that cost him reelection). Despite his integrity and impressive naval career, *that's* what folks remember about Ford: his pardon of Nixon.

That and the falling. Part of Ford's reputation as a klutz was brought on by media that turned on him after the pardon—and by a running gag in the first year of red-hot *Saturday Night Live.* But an even larger part of it was based on Ford being a klutz. He looked dumb, spoke slowly and awkwardly, tripped while getting out of Air Force One, and once hit a random person directly in the head with his ball while golfing (and also again while playing tennis). And while boarding a train after a campaign speech in Michigan, he bumped his head because he missed the door.

OFFICIAL FANTASY DREAM TEAM RATING

Ford would be a great **Moral Compass.** He pardoned Nixon because it was the right thing to do, even though he knew he would be sacrificing his own career. It's hard to find that kind of selflessness, especially in a president.

39

RONALD REAGAN

IS PROBABLY A SUPERHERO

Presidential Term: 1981–1989
Political Party: Republican
Spouses: Jane Wyman and Nancy Davis
Children: Maureen, Christine, Michael, Patti, and Ron
Birthdate: February 6, 1911
Death Date: June 5, 2004
Fun Fact: Reagan was an actor before he was president.

Viral pneumonia, diverticulosis, a cancerous colon tumor, and a close-range bullet all have one thing in common: none of them had anything to do with Ronald Reagan's death, despite them all being present in his life. In fact, even though he's the oldest man so far to hold the office of president, Reagan was also one of the fittest, and being one of the fittest on a list that includes people who juggle Indian clubs, have duels, or are Roosevelts is pretty impressive. Being strong is one thing, but Reagan displayed a unique ability to survive the kinds of things that would crush most men. It would be mildly irresponsible to suggest a definite relationship between President Ronald Reagan and fictional superhero Wolverine (who is known for his toughness, accelerated healing ability, and metal bones), but it would be reprehensible to not even *mention* the similarities. I'll just occasionally pepper in a few of the parallels in a historically responsible fashion and invite you, the reader, to draw your own conclusions.

Ronald Reagan's focus on fitness and athleticism started early; as a teenager, he worked as a lifeguard—a job that, for some reason, involved waking up every day and chopping a three-hundred-pound block of ice down into a one-hundred-pound block of ice. It's not clear *why* the particular camp where Reagan worked as a lifeguard required him to do that, but he did it seven days a week and, like Lincoln before him, used the repeated chopping motion to strengthen his arms. During his career as a lifeguard, Reagan managed to save seventy-seven lives, including one guy Reagan rescued after another lifeguard *had already given up on the man.*

Saving lives, while undeniably Wolverine-esque, isn't necessarily *specific* to Wolverine, as plenty of people save lives. So let's get into that previously mentioned bullet, because that's one of Reagan's more Wolverine-esque stories. On March 21, 1981, Reagan visited the famous Ford's Theatre in Washington, D.C. He looked at the presidential box where Lincoln had been shot and idly thought about how easily *he* could also be shot, even with all the protection surrounding modern presidents at all times. He pushed this morbid thought out of his head, shook it off, and then got shot nine days later. A mentally ill man named John Hinckley Jr. fired six shots at President Reagan on the assumption that doing so would impress actress Jodie Foster (as of this writing, it still has not). One of those bullets hit Reagan's press secretary, one hit a Secret Service agent, one hit a local cop, two missed completely, and one ricocheted off the president's car and hit Reagan's arm, bouncing off his rib, puncturing and collapsing a lung, and landing one inch from his heart. (This seems as good a time as any to reiterate that the exploding bullet *bounced* off Reagan's rib, almost as if his rib were *too strong* to be punctured, as if it were *made of adamantium, the strongest metal known to man.* While X-rays and medical professionals have never confirmed or even suggested that the former president's bones were made of adamantium, I, as a historian, am more responsible than science, so I will not callously rule it out as a possibility.) Reagan, who was hit by the bullet as he was being shoved roughly into the presidential limousine by a special agent, didn't even realize he'd been shot until he started coughing up blood a few seconds later. On the way to the hospital, Reagan lost three pints of blood.

Ronald Reagan isn't like most men. When *Reagan* got to the hospital, there wasn't a stretcher or wheelchair waiting (sidebar: what a terrible hospital), so he calmly stepped out of the car and walked into the emergency room without a problem. If you get a toy race car dislodged from your nose, they make you travel around

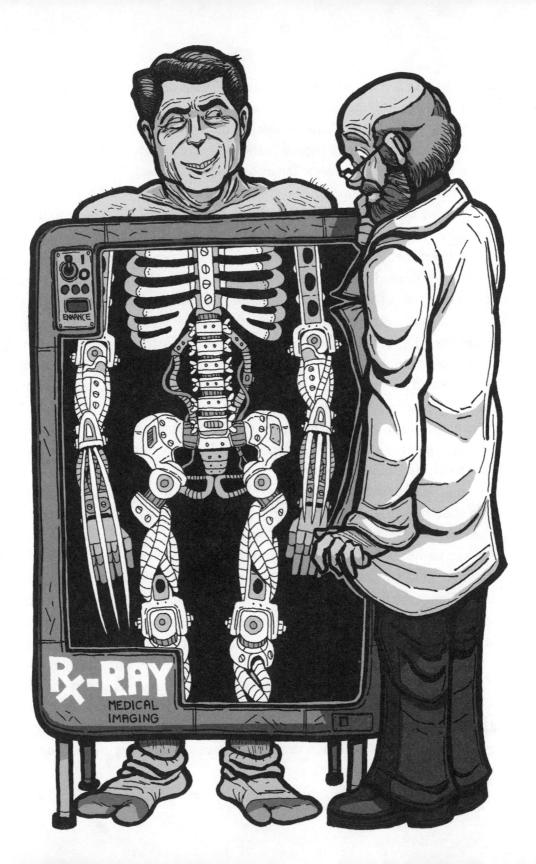

Rx-RAY
MEDICAL
IMAGING

in a wheelchair in the hospital, but Reagan, carrying on an apparent tradition of presidents who like walking around after getting shot, gets to stroll in with a bullet batting around an inch from his heart. Reagan didn't mention the bullet to the doctors; he just complained about experiencing difficulty breathing, which we can go ahead and file under "most misleading understatement ever."

Reagan's wife, Nancy, met him at the hospital and asked what had happened, to which Reagan simply replied, "Honey, I forgot to duck." He did this—smiling and cracking jokes—throughout his entire stay at the hospital, exactly like a guy who *hadn't* just been shot (or like a guy who, for argument's sake, knew that the quick recovery time afforded to him by his superhuman accelerated healing process would have him out of the hospital in no time). He was even delaying his own surgery to occasionally remove his oxygen mask and joke with the surgeons, saying, "I hope you're a Republican," after he'd *lost half of his blood and they were cutting open his body to remove the bullet.* Instead of resting after his successful surgery, Reagan stayed up all night entertaining the nurses with more jokes and anecdotes. Most seventy-year-olds would have died, but according to his doctors, Reagan had the physique of a thirty-year-old muscle builder (which, incidentally, could also be said of hit Marvel character Wolverine, should anyone out there be considering continuing comparisons between these two iconic figures).

Twelve days after he'd been shot, President Ronald Reagan went back to work. Not only that, but he used the sympathy and support his injury brought him to push the bulk of his legislation through Congress, legislation that would never have made it had he not been playing the sympathy card. Not only *that,* but he had a gym installed in the White House and gained so much muscle that he had to buy new suits. This was *after* he'd been shot. And the man was seventy years old.

Reagan's toughness, his jokes, and his easygoing nature made him one of the most relatable presidents to Americans (he carried forty-nine out of fifty states in his second election), though many of his peers and certainly leaders abroad thought the actor-turned-cowboy-president was a lot of style and very little substance. Reagan was an effective communicator unless he was mentioning facts or statistics, which he often got wrong, inspiring idiots who believed thinking with your *gut* was more important than thinking with your brain or with the assistance of facts for decades to come. Even his critics abroad, however, couldn't pretend that Reagan wasn't a major factor in ending the Cold War. In one of the most shining displays of presidential coolness, Reagan thrilled the nation in 1987 when he went to Berlin, ground zero of the Cold War and site of the infamous Berlin Wall, demanded an audience with the Soviet leader, and famously yelled, "Mr. Gorbachev, *tear down this wall!*"

Two years later the Berlin Wall fell, and with it, American fears of aggression from the Soviet Union.

(Real quick, one of Wolverine's archenemies, Omega Red, was *also* a communist. Two guys. Both hated communism. That's all I have to say—I leave it to you.)

OFFICIAL FANTASY DREAM TEAM RATING

Ronald Reagan is Wolverine. Ronald Reagan is Wolverine. Ronald Reagan is Wolverine. When the New Avengers formed, Wolverine was specifically brought in as the **Loose Cannon,** the tough, unpredictable guy who could get the job done, so it seems only fitting that Reagan serve the same purpose for you.

CONCLUSION

Now that you've reached the end of this book, you no doubt have a few questions, and I'd like to address them here.

"Would YOU ever run for president?"

Are you kidding me? Did you *read* the book? I am nowhere near as cool *or crazy* as any of the guys in this book. But you should definitely run.

"Who is your favorite president?"

It's really impossible to choose. Every time I think I'm going to pick Teddy, I get reminded of Polk's focus, or Jackson's passion, or McKinley's big ol' heart, and suddenly I find myself trying to pick ten favorites. Really, there's a great president for every mood. There's no way to choose just one.

"Who is your LEAST favorite pres—"

Richard Nixon. All day.

"Why didn't you cover living presidents?"

At the time that I am writing this book, there are five living presidents ranging in age from their fifties to their nineties. I can't really write a chapter without taking a president's entire life into account, and I didn't want to jinx any of these great men by starting a chapter while they were still alive. So in the event that we lose any of them between now and the time you're reading this book, let's all agree to imagine that they are off on some great cosmic vacation for a while, before becoming eligible to be drafted for somebody's Fantasy Dream Team. After all they've done for the country and the world, haven't they earned a break?

"Why have you dedicated so much of your life to designing Presidential Fantasy Dream Teams for a robot uprising that will never happen?"

First of all, you don't know for sure that the uprising won't happen, so don't tempt fate.

As far as why I've spent the last several years of my life reading everything

I could about presidents, that leads me to one of the more important reasons I wrote this book in the first place: to teach you that history is *much cooler* than they tell you it is in school.

Your parents, guardians, teachers, and other authority figures *kept all of history's best secrets from you.* They wanted to save the cool stuff for themselves and leave you in the dark, but I just won't stand for that.

There is a better, cooler, and COMPLETELY INSANE version of history, and your teachers have been hiding it from you all of your life for NO REASON. They want you to remember George Washington as the guy with the fake teeth who couldn't tell a lie, and they COMPLETELY LEFT OUT the cool parts about him liking the sound of bullets and being, as far as I can tell, *magic.*

I'm here to fix that. I want you to know that regardless of what you've been taught in school, the truth is so much more exciting. The best and most impressive and ridiculous stories are out there—go find them.

ACKNOWLEDGMENTS

I would like to thank my parents, Donna and Thomas O'Brien, for their relentless encouragement and for enthusiastically supporting even my dumbest ideas. You are the two best people I know.

I am thrilled to thank Charlie and Colin O'Brien, my lovely niece and nephew. I finally wrote something you'll be able to read! (Big thanks to their parents, Tommy and Dayna, too.) Thank you, David and Marne, for being real-life heroes, because it's helpful to have someone to want to be like when I grow up. My next book will be one that Walter can read.

Cody Cheshier kept me (relatively) sane during the writing of this book, and Abigail kept me company. Without the two of you . . . I mean, I won't say "I couldn't have done the book," because I *obviously* would have finished the book—I signed a contract *saying* I would, and the publisher had already paid me and everything, so I would have written it no matter what—don't be ridiculous. Still, though, you both helped me a great deal.

Thank you to Byrd Leavell, my superagent, for his guidance and protection in all things literary and for always making all my books funnier.

Thank you to Emily Easton, Samantha Gentry, and everyone else over at Crown for their patience and positivity. Emily, you are incredible. I missed literally every deadline we discussed for this book, and no one yelled at me even once. It's crazy.

Thank you to Jack O'Brien (no relation), Mandy Rusin (also no relation), and all the other amazing people at Cracked who (again) let me slack off at work while I tinkered with this.

Obviously, I couldn't have written this book without Beyoncé.

I would like to send a supersize thank-you all the way across the border to Canada to Winston Rowntree, my illustrator and friend. Thanks for making this book better, buddy. What should our next book be about?

Finally, I would like to thank every kid who picked this book up and read it all the way to the end. Never stop reading, never stop thinking. Stay curious. You are the best.

FURTHER READING AND SURFING

These lists include resources about all our presidents. Each individual president also has books and websites about them.

BOOKS

Bausum, Ann. *Our Country's Presidents: All You Need to Know About the Presidents, from George Washington to Barack Obama.* Washington, DC: National Geographic, 2013.

Calkhoven, Laurie. *I Grew Up to Be President.* New York: Scholastic, 2011.

Davis, Todd, and Marc Frey. *The New Big Book of U.S. Presidents: Fascinating Facts About Each and Every President, Including an American History Timeline.* Philadelphia: Running Press, 2013.

DeMauro, Lisa. *Presidents of the United States.* New York: HarperCollins, 2006.

Green, Dan, and Simon Basher. *U.S. Presidents: The Oval Office All-Stars!* Basher History. New York: Kingfisher, 2013.

Halbert, Patricia A., ed. *I Wish I Knew That: U.S. Presidents: Cool Stuff You Need to Know.* White Plains, NY: Reader's Digest, 2012.

Krull, Kathleen, and Kathryn Hewitt. *Lives of the Presidents: Fame, Shame (and What the Neighbors Thought).* Orlando: HMH Books for Young Readers, 2011.

Rubel, David. *Scholastic Encyclopedia of the Presidents and Their Times.* New York: Scholastic, 2009.

Stabler, David, and Doogie Horner. *Kid Presidents: True Tales of Childhood from America's Presidents.* Philadelphia: Quirk, 2014.

WEBSITES

americanhistory.si.edu/presidency/5c_frame.html
Smithsonian's National Museum of American History presents facts about the presidents and additional resources.

biography.com/people/groups/political-leaders-us-presidents
Biographies and videos about each president

britannica.com/list/5-wacky-facts-about-us-presidents
Lists five wacky facts about the birth and death of each U.S. president

history.com/topics/us-presidents
Provides biographies, speeches, videos, presidential fun facts, photo galleries, and more

historyplace.com
Includes photo galleries, audio recordings, and portraits of the presidents

kidskonnect.com/social-studies/presidents
Answers all your questions about being president, including First Ladies, biographies, quizzes, and even presidential games

kids.nationalgeographic.com/explore/history/presidential-fun-facts
List of presidential fun facts

kids.usa.gov/government/presidents/index.shtml
Provides sources to presidential libraries, national historical sites, presidential timelines, and more

millercenter.org/president
Provides facts, galleries, and essays about each president

pbskids.org/democracy/be-president
Gives the opportunity to "apply for the job" to become president for a day

pbs.org/wgbh/americanexperience/features/article-gallery/presidents-bios
Provides a short biography of each president

scholastic.com/teachers/article/timeline-guide-us-presidents
Timeline of U.S. presidents with quick facts and sources to find out more

whitehouse.gov/1600/Presidents
The White House website, with the official biography of each president

BIBLIOGRAPHY

Ambrose, Stephen E. *Eisenhower: Soldier and President.* New York: Simon & Schuster, 1990.

Beliles, Mark A., and Jerry Newcombe. *Doubting Thomas? The Religious Life and Legacy of Thomas Jefferson.* New York: Morgan James, 2015.

Bennett, William J. *America: The Last Best Hope.* Vol. I. Nashville: Thomas Nelson, 2006.

Bennett, William J., and John T. E. Cribb. *The American Patriot's Almanac: Daily Readings on America.* Nashville: Thomas Nelson, 2008.

Benson, Michael. *Ronald Reagan.* Minneapolis: Lerner, 2004.

Betts, William. *The Nine Lives of George Washington.* Bloomington, IN: iUniverse, 2013.

Boller, Paul F., Jr. *Presidential Anecdotes.* New York: Oxford University Press, 1981.

——. *Presidential Campaigns: From George Washington to George W. Bush.* New York: Oxford University Press, 2004.

——. *Presidential Diversions: Presidents at Play from George Washington to George W. Bush.* Orlando: Harcourt, 2007.

Brands, H. W. *The Man Who Saved the Union: Ulysses Grant in War and Peace.* New York: Doubleday, 2012.

Bucy, Carole Stanford. *Tennessee Through Time: The Later Years.* Layton, UT: Gibbs Smith, 2008.

Bunting, Josiah, III. *Ulysses S. Grant.* The American Presidents. New York: Times, 2004.

Burlingame, Michael. *The Inner World of Abraham Lincoln.* Urbana: University of Illinois Press, 1994.

Butt, Archibald Willingham. *Taft and Roosevelt: The Intimate Letters of Archie Butt.* Garden City, NY: Doubleday, 1930.

Caldwell, Robert Granville. *James A. Garfield, Party Chieftain.* Hamden, CT: Archon, 1965.

Conradt, Stacy. "The Last Words and Final Moments of 38 Presidents." *Mental Floss.* http://mentalfloss.com/article/51449/last -words-and-final-moments-38-presidents.

Curtis, George Ticknor. *Life of James Buchanan, Fifteenth President of the United States.* New York: Harper & Brothers, 1883.

Dallek, Robert. *Flawed Giant: Lyndon Johnson and His Times, 1961–1973.* New York: Oxford University Press, 1998.

Dalton, Kathleen. *Theodore Roosevelt: A Strenuous Life.* New York: Alfred A. Knopf, 2002.

DeGregorio, William A. *The Complete Book of U.S. Presidents, 6th Edition.* New York: Barricade Books, 2005.

DeGroot, Gerard. *The Bomb: A History of Hell on Earth.* London: Pimlico, 2005.

Dehler, Gregory J. *Chester Alan Arthur: The Life of a Gilded Age Politician and President.* First Men, America's Presidents. New York: Nova Science, 2007.

D'Este, Carlo. *Eisenhower: A Soldier's Life.* New York: Henry Holt, 2002.

Doak, Robin S. *John Tyler.* Profiles of the Presidents. Minneapolis: Compass Point, 2003.

———. *Zachary Taylor.* Profiles of the Presidents. Minneapolis: Compass Point, 2003.

Donovan, Sandy. *James Buchanan.* Presidential Leaders. Minneapolis: Lerner, 2005.

Dunn, Charles W. *The Scarlet Thread of Scandal: Morality and the American Presidency.* Lanham, MD: Rowman & Littlefield, 2000.

Edge, Laura B. *William McKinley.* Presidential Leaders. Minneapolis: Twenty-First Century, 2007.

Farwell, Byron. *Over There: The United States in the Great War, 1917–1918.* New York: Norton, 1999.

Ferling, John E. *John Adams: A Life.* Knoxville: University of Tennessee Press, 1992.

Ferrell, Robert H. *Ill-advised: Presidential Health and Public Trust.* Columbia: University of Missouri Press, 1992.

Freidel, Frank. *The Presidents of the United States of America.* Washington, DC: White House Historical Association, with the Cooperation of the National Geographic Society, 1982.

Fry, Joseph Reese. *A Life of Gen. Zachary Taylor.* Military History Series. Bedford, MA: Applewood, 1848.

Gaffney, Dennis, and Peter Gaffney. *The Presidents: Exploring History One Week at a Time.* The Seven-Day Scholar. New York: Hyperion, 2012.

Gilbert, Robert E. *The Mortal Presidency: Illness and Anguish in the White House.* New York: Basic, 1992.

Gordon-Reed, Annette. *Andrew Johnson.* The American Presidents. New York: Times, 2011.

Graff, Henry F. *Grover Cleveland.* The American Presidents. New York: Times, 2002.

Hamilton, Neil A. *Presidents: A Biographical Dictionary.* New York: Facts on File, 2001.

Harrison, James Albert. *George Washington: Patriot, Soldier, Statesman.* New York: G. P. Putnam's Sons, 1906.

Hearn, Chester G. *The Impeachment of Andrew Johnson.* Jefferson, NC: McFarland, 2000.

Henry, Mike. *What They Didn't Teach You in American History Class.* Lanham, MD: Rowman & Littlefield, 2014.

Higgs, Robert J. *God in the Stadium: Sports and Religion in America.* Lexington: University Press of Kentucky, 1995.

History Matters. "'Only Thing We Have to Fear Is Fear Itself': FDR's First Inaugural

Address." http://historymatters.gmu
.edu/d/5057.

Holmes, Jerry, ed. *Thomas Jefferson: A Chronology of His Thoughts*. Lanham, MD: Rowman & Littlefield, 2002.

Holzer, Harold. *Lincoln and the Power of the Press: The War for Public Opinion*. New York: Simon & Schuster, 2014.

Jardine, Lisa. "Lyndon B. Johnson: The Uncivil Rights Reformer." *The Independent*, January 21, 2009.

Johnson, David E., and Johnny R. Johnson. *A Funny Thing Happened on the Way to the White House: Foolhardiness, Folly, and Fraud in Presidential Elections, from Andrew Jackson to George W. Bush*. Lanham, MD: Taylor Trade, 2004.

King, David C. *Franklin Pierce*. Presidents and Their Times. Tarrytown, NY: Marshall Cavendish, 2010.

Mallon, Thomas. "Washingtonienne." Review of *Alice: Alice Roosevelt Longworth, from White House Princess to Washington Power Broker*, by Stacy A. Cordery. *New York Times*, November 18, 2007, Sunday Book Review.

Marx, Rudolph. *The Health of the Presidents*. New York: G. P. Putnam's Sons, 1960.

Mayo, Louise A. *President James K. Polk: The Dark Horse President*. First Men, America's Presidents Series. New York: Nova History, 2006.

McPherson, Stephanie Sammartino. *Theodore Roosevelt*. Presidential Leaders. Minneapolis: Lerner, 2005.

Moore, James P., Jr. *Prayer in America: A Spiritual History of Our Nation*. New York: Doubleday, 2007.

Nowlan, Robert A. *The American Presidents, Washington to Tyler: What They Did, What They Said, What Was Said About Them, with Full Source Notes*. Jefferson, NC: McFarland, 2012.

O'Boyle, Gerard. *Quotes, Jokes & Anecdotes: How to Spend Two Hours Chuckling*. Kibworth Beauchamp, UK: Matador, 2012.

O'Brien, Michael. *John F. Kennedy: A Biography*. New York: Thomas Dunne, 2005.

Peskin, Allan. *Garfield: A Biography*. Kent, OH: Kent State University Press, 1978.

Pine, Joslyn T., ed. *Wit and Wisdom of the American Presidents: A Book of Quotations*. Mineola, NY: Dover, 2001.

Powaski, Ronald E. *Toward an Entangling Alliance: American Isolationism, Internationalism, and Europe, 1901–1950*. New York: Greenwood, 1991.

Rawley, James A. *Abraham Lincoln and a Nation Worth Fighting For*. Wheeling, IL: Harlan Davidson, 1996.

Ray, James Lee. *American Foreign Policy and Political Ambition*. Washington, DC: CQ, 2008.

Russell, Francis. *The Shadow of Blooming Grove: Warren G. Harding in His Times*. New York: McGraw-Hill, 1968.

Schnakenberg, Robert. *Distory: A Treasury of Historical Insults*. New York: St. Martin's, 2004.

Schneider, Dorothy, and Carl J. Schneider. *First Ladies: A Biographical Dictionary*. New York: Facts on File, 2001.

Schroeder-Lein, Glenna R., and Richard Zuczek. *Andrew Johnson: A Biographical Companion*. Santa Barbara, CA: ABC-CLIO, 2001.

Stead, W. T. *The Review of Reviews*. Vol. 13. London: Office of the Review of Reviews, 1896.

Thornton, Brian. *The Everything Kids' Presidents Book: Puzzles, Games, and Trivia—for Hours of Presidential Fun!* Avon, MA: Adams Media, 2007.

Updegrove, Mark K. *Second Acts: Presidential Lives and Legacies After the White House*. Guilford, CT: Lyons, 2006.

U.S. Diplomacy Center. *Voices of U.S. Diplomacy and the Berlin Wall*. President Ronald Reagan. http://diplomacy.state.gov /berlinwall/www/exhibitions/tear-down -this-wall.html.

Van Buren, Martin. "First Inaugural Address—Teaching American History." Teaching American History. http://teachingamericanhistory.org /library/document/first-inaugural -address-13

Vigdor, Jacob L. *From Immigrants to Americans: The Rise and Fall of Fitting In*. Lanham, MD: Rowman & Littlefield, 2009.

Vile, John R., William D. Pederson, and Frank J. Williams, eds. *James Madison: Philosopher, Founder, and Statesman*. Athens: Ohio University Press, 2008.

Wallace, Chris. *Character: Profiles in Presidential Courage*. New York: Rugged Land, 2004.

Walters, Ryan S. *The Last Jeffersonian: Grover Cleveland and the Path to Restoring the Republic*. Bloomington, IN: WestBow, 2012.

Wasserman, Benny. *Presidents Were Teenagers Too*. Victoria, BC: Trafford, 2006.

Wheelan, Joseph. *Mr. Adams's Last Crusade: John Quincy Adams's Extraordinary Post-presidential Life in Congress*. New York: PublicAffairs, 2008.

Wilson, Douglas L., and Rodney O. Davis, eds. *Herndon's Informants: Letters, Interviews, and Statements About Abraham Lincoln*. Urbana: University of Illinois Press, 1998.

SOURCE NOTES

George Washington
"I heard the bullets whistle . . ." Harrison, 77
"I am just going," Betts, 144

John Adams
"the Atlas of American Independence." Ferling, 150

Thomas Jefferson
"Thomas Jefferson still survives." Holmes, 308
"Here was buried Thomas Jefferson, . . ." Beliles and Newcombe, 187

James Madison
"You will now leave the room . . ." Boller, *Presidential Diversions*, 43
"frail and discernibly fragile appearance . . ." Vile, Pederson, and Williams, 22

John Quincy Adams
"butchered in cold blood, . . ." DeGregorio, 92
"whole life [had] been a succession . . ." Wheelan, 103

Andrew Jackson
"rattled like a bag of marbles" Wallace, 80
"grand passion" Nowlan, 254
"resort to petty and vindictive acts . . ." ibid.
"I didn't shoot Henry Clay . . ." Schnakenberg, 78

Martin Van Buren
"laced up in corsets, . . ." Johnson and Johnson, 25
"I must go into the presidential chair . . ." Van Buren

William Henry Harrison
"Let no committee, . . ." Johnson and Johnson, 4
"By my sword, . . ." DeGregorio, 140

John Tyler
"eight dozen bottles . . ." Boller, *Presidential Diversions*, 80
"I am going. . . ." Doak, *John Tyler*, 49

James K. Polk
"a more ridiculous, contemptible, . . ." Holzer, 65
"supervise the whole operations . . ." Mayo, 71
"shed American blood . . ." Ray, 45
"early physical inferiority," DeGregorio, 163

Zachary Taylor
"Taylor never surrenders!" Fry, 26
"enter the head of any sane person." Doak, *Zachary Taylor*, 38
"with less reluctance . . ." Freidel, 30

Millard Fillmore
"the Know-Nothings get control," Vigdor, 32
"no man should, in my judgment, . . ." Boller, *Presidential Anecdotes*, 112

Franklin Pierce
"This is the last great battle . . ." King, 61
"The only thing left to do . . ." Boller, *Presidential Diversions*, 100

James Buchanan
"I acknowledge no master . . ." Pine, 24
"It is now no time for explanation, . . ." Curtis, 18

"pints," Buchanan wrote, "are very inconvenient . . ." Donovan, 81

Abraham Lincoln
"Who is dead in the White House?" Rawley, 220
"to give his proboscis . . ." Burlingame, 151
"one thousand pounds," Wilson and Davis, 13
"if you heard his fellin' trees . . ." Stead, 54

Andrew Johnson
"The Vice President Elect . . ." Henry, 76
"I kiss this Book . . ." Gordon-Reed, 85
"Honest conviction is my courage," Schroeder-Lein and Zuczek, 339
"any one who talks of surrender . . ." Hearn, 25
"remarkable for its incoherence," Moore, 186
"one of bitter contempt and aversion" Gaffney and Gaffney, 137
"no friend of our race." ibid.

Ulysses S. Grant
"Treat the negro as a citizen . . ." Brands, 548
"the original inhabitants" Bunting, 117
"the whole race would be harmless . . ." ibid., 118

Rutherford B. Hayes
"he continued to give direction . . ." DeGregorio, 228
"an unusual strength . . ." Marx, 238
"fighting battles is like . . ." DeGregorio, 290
"Good God! Has it come . . ." Johnson and Johnson, 49

James Garfield
"made the ridicule and . . ." Peskin, 9
"refused to obey" Caldwell, 22

Chester A. Arthur
"When Chester was a boy, . . ." Dehler, 3

Grover Cleveland
"If we expect to become great . . ." Wasserman, 75

"A public office is a public trust," Graff, 82
"[h]e had no endowments . . ." Walters, xviii
"Now, Jerry, I want you . . ." Schneider and Schneider, 143
"I have tried so hard to do right." Conradt
"gelatinous mound" Ferrell, 7
Frances said, "four years." DeGregorio, 323
"ham-like," ibid., 319

Benjamin Harrison
"Now I walk with God." Hamilton, 196
by Theodore Roosevelt as "cold-blooded" DeGregorio, 341
"Then let God reelect you" Boller, *Presidential Campaigns*, 165

William McKinley
"Don't let them hurt him" Edge, 8

Theodore Roosevelt
"nobody seemed to think . . ." Dalton, 35
"man does in fact become fearless . . ." ibid., 52
"It will be awful . . ." Higgs, 160
"The bullet is in me now." McPherson, 95
"the mind but . . . not the body, . . ." Gaffney and Gaffney, 160
"who has in him . . ." Boller, *Presidential Anecdotes*, 196

William Howard Taft
"politics make me sick," Butt, 295

Woodrow Wilson
"impulsive, passionate, . . ." DeGregorio, 409
". . . dormant volcano, placid on the outside, . . ." ibid.
"contracted [Wilson's] usually relaxed . . ." Marx, 315

Warren G. Harding
"Teddy Roosevelt's daughter" Mallon
"with being 'a liar, . . .'" Russell, 92

Calvin Coolidge
"in a state of constant anxiety" Gilbert, 39

"[t]hose who saw Coolidge in a rage . . ." ibid.
"men do what I tell them to do." ibid., 28

Herbert Hoover
"Turn your cheek once," Thornton, 90
"more strenuous than . . ." Boller, *Presidential Diversions*, 224
"Work is life." Powaski, 50

Franklin Delano Roosevelt
"the one person I ever knew, . . ." DeGregorio, 503
"If you ever spent two years in bed . . ." Marx, 363
"this nation asks for action, . . ." History Matters

Harry S. Truman
"Boys, if you ever pray, . . ." Bucy, 244
"we have discovered . . ." DeGroot, 80
"I never heard a man cuss . . ." Farwell, 224

Dwight D. Eisenhower
"How many times . . ." Ambrose, 479
"lots of troubles . . ." D'Este, 209
"I want to go. . . ." Updegrove, 49

"never lost a soldier . . ." DeGregorio, 542
"refused to get in a . . ." Bennett, 408

John F. Kennedy
"There's nothing in the book . . ." O'Brien, 147
"You can't say that Dallas . . ." ibid., 903
"play [a sport] unless you . . ." Gilbert, 143
"to crowd as much . . ." ibid., 162
"when he loses." Gaffney and Gaffney, 235

Lyndon B. Johnson
"I knew from the start . . ." Dallek, 246
"get up every day . . ." Jardine

Richard Nixon
"lied to gain love, . . ." Dunn, 129
"We'll just slip them . . ." Gaffney and Gaffney, 269
"called no good" O'Boyle, 165

Ronald Reagan
"Honey, I forgot to duck." Bennett and Cribb, 99
"I hope you're a Republican," Benson, 82
"Mr. Gorbachev, tear down this wall!" U.S. Diplomacy Center

INDEX